KIEV

ARCHITECTURAL LANDMARKS
AND ART MUSEUMS

**AN
ILLUSTRATED
GUIDE**

Aurora Art Publishers · Leningrad

Compiled by SEMION GUROK
and BORIS LOBANOVSKY

Designed by VALERY LUZHIN

Layout by NIKOLAI KUTOVOI

Translated from the Russian
by ANNE STAROS

Photographs by
ROMAN BENIAMINSON,
YURI BUSLENKO,
IGOR KROPIVNITSKY,
BORIS MINDEL,
VALERY MORUZHENKO,
NIKOLAI RAKHMANOV,
VADIM SOLOVSKY,
TARAS SHABLOVSKY
and VASILY SHCHERBAKOV

K $\dfrac{4902020000\text{-}366}{023(01)\text{-}87}$ 1-86

CONTENTS

THE UKRAINIAN SOVIET
SOCIALIST REPUBLIC

Kiev

Kharkov

Lvov

Odessa

Simferopol

Frunze St.

3

Krasnykh
Kazakov
Prospekt

2

4

Pobedy Prospekt

6

1

7

Vozdukhoflotsky Prospekt

8

Vladimirskaya St.

Sorokaletiya Oktiabria Prospekt

14

15

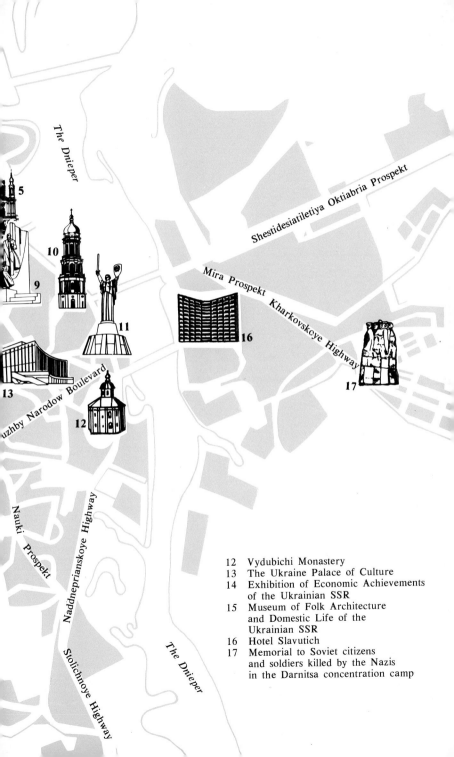

The Dnieper

Shestidesiatiletiya Oktiabria Prospekt

Mira Prospekt

Kharkovskoye Highway

uzhby Narodow Boulevard

Nauki Prospekt

Naddneprianskoye Highway

Stolichnoye Highway

The Dnieper

5

10

9

11

13

12

16

17

12   Vydubichi Monastery
13   The Ukraine Palace of Culture
14   Exhibition of Economic Achievements
     of the Ukrainian SSR
15   Museum of Folk Architecture
     and Domestic Life of the
     Ukrainian SSR
16   Hotel Slavutich
17   Memorial to Soviet citizens
     and soldiers killed by the Nazis
     in the Darnitsa concentration camp

Kiev, the capital of the Soviet Ukraine, is one of the oldest cities of Eastern Europe. It is situated on the hilly right bank and on the low left bank of the Dnieper River. Inimitable in the beauty and variety of its green landscape, a garden city, a city of museums, the Kiev of today is one of the largest industrial, scientific and cultural centres of the Soviet Union.

During the past few decades, the area of the third largest city in the USSR (after Moscow and Leningrad) has increased by more than one and a half times. Including the new Levoberezhye (Left Bank) residential areas, by 1980 it had reached 782 square kilometres. Every year new regions rise up, and ensembles original in their architectural conception are created.

The cultural achievements of Kiev's inhabitants are considerable. The city is often the site of art festivals and exhibitions; many films are shot there and a large number of books published. Music lovers abroad have more than once had the opportunity to assess the exceptional skill of Kiev's Philharmonic musicians. Not only in the Soviet Union but also beyond its borders, the musical comedies of the Ivan Franko Ukrainian Theatre enjoy invariable success.

The steep hills of the Pravoberezhye (Right Bank), the green islands on the Dnieper, and the wide expanses of the steppe on the left bank retain the traces of thousands of years of the past. Archaeological finds, uncovered here at different times, reflect all the stages of the ancient history of the central Dnieper River Basin. Archaeological data as well as the chronicles of Byzantine, Armenian and Arabian historians indicate that Kiev was founded in the late fifth or early sixth century, which was a period of great unrest on the part of the Slavic tribes, when their forces moved beyond the Danube, invaded the territory of the Byzantine Empire, and their boats appeared at the walls of Constantinople itself. At this same time, a settlement arose on the northern spur of Old Kiev Hill.

A legend mentioned in eleventh-century chronicles tells of how the brothers Kiy, Shchek, Khoriv and their sister Lybed founded a city on the heights above the Dnieper and named it after the oldest brother — Kiev. All the most important events of the city's history are linked with the Upper Town — Old Kiev — and Old Kiev Hill. Protected by this hill, at the mouth of the Pochaina River, lay a well-sheltered harbour for boats sailing along the Dnieper. Here the other part of ancient Kiev — Podol (Lower Town) — developed, inhabited by merchants and craftsmen.

By the ninth century Kiev was already a populous trading centre. The most important trade route, the route "from the Varangians to the Greeks", from the Baltic (Varangian) Sea to the Black Sea, passed through it following the three northern rivers, the Neva, Volkhov and Lovat, and the Dnieper and linking the Slavic lands with the Byzantine Empire.

The rise of the city contributed to the unification of the Eastern Slavic lands. The first ancient Russian chronicle (*svod*), *The Tale of Bygone Years*, contains the story of the capture of Kiev in 882 by Novgorod hosts led by their Prince Oleg and of the murder of the local Princes Askold and Dir. At the foot of Ugorsk Hill, where these events were played out, is Askold's Tomb. The victor together with Igor, the young son of the Novgorod Prince Rurik, settled within the fortifications on Old Kiev Hill, having proclaimed Kiev their capital, "the mother of all Russian cities".

In the middle of the tenth century, construction in the Upper Town began to extend beyond the limits of the old fortifications. Two stone palaces of Princess Olga, the wife and widow of Igor, were erected at this time, one in the town, the other outside it. Judging by the archaeological excavations of 1970—72, the interior of the first palace was decorated with pilasters, paintings on limestone plaster and majolica tiles.

During the reign of Prince Vladimir Sviatoslavich (980—1015), the Kiev *detinets* (an archaic Russian word meaning inner fortress, or citadel of the reigning prince), located in the Upper Town, also expanded. In a series of campaigns, the Prince gradually completed the process of unification of the Eastern Slavic principalities. The resulting intensive construction in the city corresponded with the new problems of centralization. The defensive fortifications of Vladimir City enclosed an area of exactly 10 hectares. In 1240, the St. Sophia Gate (or the Batu Gate), opening onto the descent into Podol and toward the fields outside the city, became the last stronghold of the defenders of Kiev against the Tatar-Mongol hordes.

To the north of the present-day upper station of the Funicular, Perun Hill was located, a pagan sanctuary with pillar-like statues of the gods of ancient Slavs.

The struggle of the Kiev Prince to unite ancient Russia demanded the establishment of a state religion that could prevail over local pagan cults. The adoption of Christianity in 988 was thus an important political and cultural act. The new religion not only reinforced the authority of feudal power, but also brought with it the wisdom of the written word, introducing the culture of the Byzantine Empire into the young Kievan state. At this point, the character of the buildings in Kiev changed fundamentally. On the highest part of the plateau, in the centre of the *detinets* in the City of Vladimir, the first stone church in Russia, the Church of the Holy Virgin, was constructed. Vladimir granted a tenth of his income for its upkeep, so that it came later to be known as the Church of the Tithe (Desiatinnaya). Experienced Byzan-

tine stone-masons worked quickly. The three-aisled cruciform church, whose foundation stone was laid down in 989, was completed in seven years. Because of the abundance of marble details and columns, people called it "the marble church". Unfortunately, it did not survive the 1240 siege of the city by the Tatar-Mongol hordes. It collapsed under the blows of the wall-crushing siege weapons. The outline of its foundation, now laid with red quartzite, helps us to visualize the floor plan of the church. Fragments of frescoes, mosaics and slate bas-reliefs testify to the rich decoration of its interior. The western façade of the church faced the rectangular building of a palace, erected in the tenth or eleventh century. Judging by the width of the pillars and the thickness of the walls, the building had two stories. Another small palace with two lateral towers stood to the south of the church. The square in front of the church received the name of Women's Market. An antique bronze quadriga that used to stand there had been brought from the Crimean city of Korsun (Chersones) in 988 as a war trophy by Prince Vladimir. Not far from the Church of the Tithe rose the cupolas of several more churches: the St. Andrew and St. Theodore monastery churches, the St. Basil Church and the Church of the Exaltation of the Cross.

Since the nineteenth century a large number of articles from the eleventh to thirteenth centuries, which were hidden away during the Tatar-Mongol invasion, have been unearthed in this area.

The rule of the son of Prince Vladimir, Prince Yaroslav the Wise

(1019—54), was the apex of the flowering of ancient Kiev. The area of the Upper Town increased by more than seven times. The high ramparts of the City of Yaroslav, consisting of several rows of wooden frames, filled with earth, encircled Old Kiev Hill. The central street of the city, which followed, with only slight variation, the path of present-day Vladimirskaya Street, connected the St. Sophia Gate of Vladimir's City with the new Golden Gate. The latter showed a certain affinity with *Porta Aurea* in Constantinople. The Church of the Annunciation built over this gate was surmounted by a stone tower. The Golden Gate was not only the main entrance into Kiev, but also the most heavily fortified entrance. Not far away, along the central street, monasteries were located with their stone churches of St. Gregory and St. Irene, the patron saints of the Prince's family. The Palace was built alongside the monastery of St. Irene (present-day Irininskaya Street). The entire ensemble of stone and wooden buildings was dom-

inated by thirteen-domed St. Sophia's Cathedral, the main cathedral of the Russian Metropolitan. The street on its east side led to the northwest Lvov Gate (located on present-day Lvov Square) with a stone tower over it. Beyond this gate lay the vast mercantile suburb of Kiev — Kopyrev End. On the opposite side of the Old Kiev plateau, over wooded

slopes of the Kreshchatik Stream valley, towered the Liadskiye Gate. This gate, connected with dramatic events of the siege of Kiev by the Tatar-Mongol forces, stood where Kalinin Street runs today. The Liadskiye Gate was directly connected with the princely estate of Berestovo and the Pechersky (Cave) Monastery.
The fortification of the Upper Town was completed during the

1. The outline of the foundation of an eleventh-century Prince's palace

2. Model showing Kiev in the twelfth century

13

reigns of Prince Iziaslav and his son Sviatopolk in the second half of the eleventh and early twelfth century.

On Mikhailovsky Hill, where present-day Parizhskoy Kommuny (Paris Commune) Street intersects with Kalinin Square, St. Demetrius's Monastery was constructed, comprising several stone churches — St. Demetrius's Cathedral (1060s), Cathedral of St. Michael of the Golden Cupolas (1108—13) and the Church of St. Peter (1070s).

Western writers of that time described Kiev as one of the major cities of the world. The German chronicler, Thietmar Merseburgensis, wrote that in Kiev there were 400 churches, eight market squares and countless numbers of people. Another prominent monastic author, Adalbert von Bremen, called the capital of Kievan Rus "a rival to the sceptre of Constantinople". It is unlikely that these accounts are merely exaggeration.

According to modern archaeological data, the central territory occupied by Kiev during the twelfth century consisted of more than 380 hectares. Judging by the number of private dwelling houses in the city, its population numbered no less than 50,000 people, which exceeded the population of the majority of Europe's great cities at that time.

From the second half of the twelfth century well into the thirteenth century, Kiev was the scene of numerous fierce battles between rival princes. This feudal strife led to the weakening of the unity of the ancient Russian state.

In the autumn of 1240, Tatar-Mongol forces, numbering more than 149 thousand, under the leadership of Khan Batu were amassed outside the walls of Kiev. After a ten-week assault on the city, the Liadskiye Gate was destroyed; the same fate awaited the St. Sophia Gate and the Church of the Tithe. The last defenders of the city, women and children, died under the collapsing roof of this church.

In the flames of the fires perished Kiev's splendid palaces and churches, and the priceless library of Prince Yaroslav the Wise. Excavations of these ashen remains, as well as thousands of mass graves and secret caves where the city's survivors hid themselves, reveal for us the traces of bitter struggle.

After the Tatar-Mongol invasion, life in the Upper Town virtually died out for a period of several centuries. Today, only the Cathedral of St. Sophia and the ruins of the Golden Gate remain from those times, a small part of Kiev's imposing architectural ensembles of the tenth to thirteenth centuries.

The centre of Kiev moved gradually down to Podol. The frequent fires and the constant fear of the Tatar-Mongol invasions hampered construction. During the following period of Lithuanian and Polish domination, Kiev's buildings were solely of wood. Only in the second quarter of the seventeenth century a few stone buildings began to goup. After the Ukraine reunited with Russia in 1654, construction assumed an ever larger scope. From this moment architects from St. Petersburg and Moscow co-operated with Ukrainian masters in creating Kiev's new architectural ensembles.

From the end of the seventeenth century to the mid-eighteenth century,

a style known as Ukrainian Baroque predominated in the construction of Kiev. Decorative motifs derived from Ukrainian folk art and from wooden structures were widely used in the city's architecture.

In the middle of the eighteenth century, the influence of the Petersburg school of Late Baroque manifested itself in Kiev, due in large part to the work on the Church of St. Andrew and the Tsar's Palace, designed by

3. The outline of the foundation of the Church of the Tithe

15

St. Petersburgian architects. In sharp contrast to these buildings are the more elegant though simple structures put up by local architects at the Kievo-Pecherskaya Lavra and Podol.

With the development of modern systems of town planning in the late eighteenth and early nineteenth century projects for the planned building of Kiev appeared. The riverbed of the dried up Kreshchatik Stream became the most important street in the city, as roads ran to it from the Upper Town, Podol and Pechersk.

Strict and imposing Classical forms dominated the architecture of the early nineteenth century, evident in such constructions as the University and buildings on Kontraktovaya Square (now Red Square) in Podol. In the following period the character of construction in the centre of Kiev changed; on the main streets in a continuous line stretched the façades of elegant private residences, banks and hotels. The external decoration of these buildings depended not so much on the architect's design or on the style which ought to be in accordance with the general appearance of a street or square, as on the personal taste of the client.

Features of Art Nouveau, a style which predominated in early twentieth-century Kievan architecture, are very distinctly manifested in the extravagant house of the architect Vladislav Gorodetsky in Pechersk, built according to his own design in 1902—3.

In reaction to the decorative fantasies of Art Nouveau, Neoclassicism became popular. Characteristic features of this stern, rational style are reflected in bank buildings in Kreshchatik and in a number of ensembles put up in Pechersk just before the First World War.

With the victory of the October Revolution, conditions were provided for the development of Ukrainian national culture. Construction began on housing, new industrial centres and workers' clubs. The accent on rational, well-planned architectural projects using new building materials and on expressive and clear form culminated in a series of noteworthy architectural ensembles of the 1920s and early '30s.

In 1934, Kiev became the capital of the Soviet Ukraine, which triggered a period of intensive construction. A far-reaching plan for reconstruction of the city envisioned the creation of industrial and administrative cenetrs, comfortable, well-appointed living quarters and large sports facilities. Again there was renewed interest in Neoclassicism.

The realization of these plans was interrupted by the Great Patriotic War (1941—45). Immeasurable destruction was caused to Kiev by the Nazi occupation forces. More than 195 thousand people, inhabitants of Kiev and Soviet Army soldiers and officers, were either brutally murdered at Baby Yar or tortured in the concentration camps at Darnitsa and Syrets. Over two thousand factories, public buildings and apartment houses, and many outstanding architectural monuments were destroyed. The magnificent eleventh-century Cathedral of the Dormition was blown up, and nearly thirty other buildings of the Kievo-Pecherskaya Lavra were turned into rubble. The main building of the University was set afire. Kreshchatik and other central streets lay in ruins.

After liberation of the city by the Soviet Army in November 1943, Kiev rose from the ruins anew. Leading architects from all over the country took part in a competition for the best project of reconstruction of Kreshchatik in late 1944. Architects designing the new ensemble of the city's main artery took into account its hilly relief. High-rise apartment buildings on the left-hand side of Kreshchatik give it a highly expressive outline.

In 1945, construction began on another city thoroughfare, the Druzhby Narodov (International Friendship) Boulevard, entering the city from the side of Moscow, Leningrad and Kharkov.

Architecture of the first post-war decade is typified by a very decorative style and by wide use of forms and devices characteristic of Baroque and Neoclassicism. However, by the second half of the 1950s this tendency had undergone changes; these were a noticeable striving toward simplicity and concern to achieve the organic unity of a building's function and its architectural form. Greater attention was given to comfort and modern amenities in the design of housing units. Monumental decorative art began to play a significant role in Kiev's architectural planning; statues of writers, composers, artists, revolutionary and war heroes and prominent political figures began to be erected in parks and squares throughout the city. Memorials at Darnitsa, Baby Yar, and in the Park of Eternal Glory, as well as the Ukrainian Museum of the History of the Great Patriotic War are continual reminders of the suffering under the Nazis and the heroic victory of the Soviet peoples.

The Upper Town

1 St. Sophia: Museum Complex of History and Architecture
2 Monument to Bogdan Khmelnitsky
3 Church of St. Andrew
4 Pavilion over the Golden Gate
5 Monument to Prince Vladimir Sviatoslavich
6 Monument to the Baptism of Russia and the Return of the *Magdeburger Recht* to Kiev
7 Refectory-type church of the Monastery of St. Michael of the Golden Cupolas
8 University
9 Monument to Taras Shevchenko
10 Opera and Ballet House and the statue of the Ukrainian composer Nikolai Lysenko
11 Cathedral of St. Vladimir

Traditionally, acquaintance with Kiev's architectural monuments begins with the **Cathedral of St. Sophia,** one of the buildings making up the **St. Sophia Museum Complex of History and Architecture.** It is located at the junction of Vladimirskaya Street and Bogdan Khmelnitsky Square, where it dominates all the surrounding buildings, lending its distinctive air not only to the square's architectural ensemble but to the whole Upper Town.

Passing through the entrance gate of the tall Bell Tower, we reach this imposing structure, founded in 1037 by Yaroslav the Wise (1019—54). The construction of the main cathedral and fortifications of Yaroslav's City was preceded by important historical events. The sudden death of Mstislav, the militant rival prince of Chernigov, made Yaroslav the supreme sovereign of Russian lands. The victory in 1036 of Yaroslav's forces over the Pecheneg host on the field before the Kiev *detinets* ensured peace on the southern frontiers of the state. Therefore, it was under Yaroslav's rule that particularly intensive building work took place.

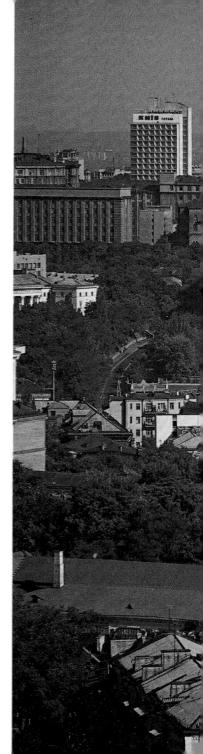

The central monumental religious structure of Yaroslav's Kiev and the greatest achievement of Kievan Rus, the Cathedral of St. Sophia (Cathedral of the Holy Wisdom) was built in honour of decisive victory over Pechenegs. The very idea of its creation was an indication of the mature political and cultural role of Kievan Rus. The dedication of the cathedral to St. Sophia showed the desire of Prince Yaroslav to pattern the Russian capital after Constantinople. In his reign, other cities of Ancient Rus also built Cathedrals

4. Bogdan Khmelnitsky Square

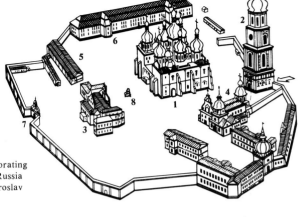

5. Plan of the St. Sophia Monastery

1 St. Sophia Cathedral
2 Bell Tower
3 Metropolitan's house
4 Refectory-type church (Wart St. Sophia's)
5 Brethren's House
6 Seminary
7 Zaborovsky (West) Gate
8 Granite stele commemorating the first library in Old Russia founded by Prince Yaroslav the Wise

of St. Sophia, for instance, Novgorod (1045—50) and Polotsk (1044—66).

St. Sophia's was one of the largest buildings in Europe in mid-eleventh century. In terms of interior decoration, its large areas of mosaic and frescoes place it well ahead of all known monuments of its time.

Kievan St. Sophia's was a thirteen-domed, five-aisled cathedral with two stair-towers and two one-storey arcades. In plan it measures 37 by 55 metres; its height, including the main cupola, is 29 metres. It was designed to fulfil the functions of a central state temple, namely, as the seat of the Russian Metropolitan, as a people's forum and as a place for court ceremonies.

The cathedral had a festive appearance. The walls were laid of flat bricks set in a mixture of slaked lime with fine pinkish brick dust. Thin half-columns ornamented the cupola drums and apses. Shallow niches accenting the rhythmical divisions of the façade contained frescoes of saints and Christian symbols. Bright ornaments embellished the supports of the open arcades. The main entrance had a portico with marble columns. The half-spherical cupolas and *zakomary* (semicircular upper sections of outer walls, covering the adjoining cylindrical inner vaults and reflecting their shape) were covered with lead sheets with delicate ornamental engraving. The central dome was gilded. In spite of the fact that the basic portion of the building has been well preserved, the current aspect of St. Sophia's is quite different from the original structure. The arcades have been bricked up and the cupolas assumed a helmet-like form typical of Baroque and increased to nineteen. Repairs which were undertaken in 1848—63 have changed the type of St. Sophia's roofing as well as the composition of the cathedral's west façade.

The interior of the cathedral has preserved its eleventh-century aspect. Its decoration is closely coupled with the architecture and is perceived as one artistic whole. Mosaic, as the most durable and dear material, is used in the most important places in the Cathedral — in the central apse, on the four supporting arches of the central dome, on the pendentives, and in the central dome. Especially bright was the mosaic floor under the central dome. Other areas of the walls were painted with frescoes.

On entering the cathedral, the viewer does not notice the mosaics and paintings on the lower parts of the walls. The eye is immediately drawn to the central dome. There, in a golden glow of mosaic, Christ Pantocrator looks down on us, monumental and severe, framed in a medallion (di-

6. St. Sophia's
Cathedral.
View from the east

7. Central nave
of St. Sophia's
Cathedral

ameter 4.1. metres). This artistic
embodiment of the ethereal and
earthly hierarchy corresponded to
the worldview of the man of the
Middle Ages.

The sparkling mosaics of the
chancel apse occupy the central
position in the cathedral. In the
concha is an enormous (about 6
metres high) figure of the Virgin
Orans, called the Indestructible
Wall, the patron saint of Kiev and
of the whole state. Under the
Orans, divided from her by an ornamental frieze, the scene of the
Eucharist — the apostles receiv-
ing the sacrament of Holy Com-
munion — is depicted. Further

8. St. Sophia's Cathedral. *Christ Pantocrator*

9. St. Sophia's Cathedral. Dome of the choir

10. St. Sophia's Cathedral. *The Archangel Gabriel* from the *Annunciation*

11. St. Sophia's Cathedral. *The Virgin* from the *Annunciation*

down is one of the most monumental of St. Sophia's mosaics, a group of eight bishops and two archdeacons.

Though the arrangement of the cathedral's paintings is quite traditional, there are some variations. The mosaics in the central dome and chancel are organically bound to the frescoes, which are greater in number. The contrast of the shining golden ground in the mosaics and the blues in the frescoes reflects the transition from the ethereal symbols to the narrative subjects of the scenes devoted to Christ's earthly life. These are painted on the vaults

12. St. Sophia's Cathedral. Family
of Prince Yaroslav the Wise

and walls of that part of the Cathedral where the main nave intersected the transcept. The originality of St. Sophia's frescoes lies in the number of secular subjects. The family portraits of Yaroslav the Wise occupied three walls on the western side of the central

nave. The portrayal of the princely couple during their lifetime in the central section of the Cathedral was extremely rare in medieval artistic practice. This was connected with the tendency to deify the princely ruler. The central part of the composition depicting Yaro-slav and his wife was obliterated when a three-centred arch under the choir was dismantled in the eighteenth century. The frescoes on the north wall of the nave were painted later. Only a small fragment of the eleventh-century fresco with the portrait of one of the princely offsprings has survived. And of the south wall paintings only the figures of the children of Yaroslav the Wise have come down to us.

Exceptionally interesting are the frescoes in the stair-towers of the Cathedral, which have practically no equivalents among surviving examples of early medieval monumental painting. These frescoes, with their secular subjects, did not reproduce compositions which used to beautify the private quarters of Byzantine emperors, but developed the local tradition of embellishing tenth- and eleventh-century Kiev palaces with mural paintings and mosaic panels. This tradition is most evident in scenes of royal hunts (*The Bear Hunt, Coursing after Squirrels, Attack of an Enraged Animal*, representation of birds trained for hunting, etc.), which have much in common with descriptions of the hunt occurring in Prince Vladimir Monomachus's autobiographical *Instruction*. The representations of buffoons and musicians from the cycle of frescoes painted in the south tower also reflect aspects of everyday life, already familiar from the

chronicles. The large composition in the south tower, representing the imperial box and a chariot race at the Constantinople Hippodrome, is rich in homely details which could be detected only by an eye-witness. One of the most prominent Soviet scholars, Victor Lasarev, in comparing the individual manner of mosaic artists, concluded that no less than eight

experienced masters worked in St. Sophia's. All but one, however, remain anonymous. The exception, Georgy, left his name in Greek on the wall of the Cathedral. The work was completed in three years. It consisted of about 640 square metres of mosaic (260 square metres have survived), with about nine million smalt tesserae. The palette of the mosaic is distinguished by its variety. Thirty-four of the 177 basic hues are comprised of gold and silver smalts, which are imparting the unusual intensity to the golden ground.

The rhythm of the multicoloured ornaments on the arches and walls

13, 14. *The Eucharist* from the Monastery of St. Michael of the Golden Cupolas.
St. Sophia: Museum Complex of History and Architecture

15. St. Sophia's Cathedral. *The Eucharist.* Detail

is in happy accordance with the severe carving of the slate slabs serving as a railing of the choir gallery. In the eleventh century, carpet-like patterns on the floor, encrusted with mosaic and marble, were added to this impressive ensemble.

In order to lighten the ceiling and create good acoustics in the cathedral, clay vessels (resonators) were immured in the vaults.

In the decoration of the gallery interiors multicoloured ceramic tiles play a large role.

By the accounts of travellers who visited Kiev in the late sixteenth century, St. Sophia's still retained its former majesty. The cathedral was compared favourably with magnificent St. Sophia's in Constantinople and with the splendid cathedrals of Venice.

The tomb of Yaroslav the Wise, located in the north (St. Vladimir) chapel of the cathedral, is the most ancient and unique carved marble monument extant. Its surface is decorated with early Christian symbols: stylized representations of palms, cypresses, fish and grapevines. The sarcophagus was carved in the Near East,

16. *St. George* and *St. Theodore Stratelates* from the Monastery of St. Michael of the Golden Cupolas. St. Sophia: Museum Complex of History and Architecture

17. St. Sophia's Cathedral. *Buffoons*

18. *The Archbishop Stephen* from the Monastery of St. Michael of the Golden Cupolas. St. Sophia: Museum Complex of History and Architecture

19. Tomb of Prince Yaroslav the Wise. St. Sophia: Museum Complex of History and Architecture

20. West façade
of St. Sophia's
Cathedral

21. The Metropolitan's
house at St. Sophia's
Monastery

22. Lower part
of the Bell Tower
in the St. Sophia
Monastery

sometime during the fifth or sixth century, then brought to Kiev, where it became in 1054 the tomb for Prince Yaroslav the Wise and his wife Irine. Exhibited in the north (external) gallery of the cathedral is a sculptural portrait of the prince which was reconstructed from his skull by the well-known Soviet scholar and sculptor-anthropologist, Mikhail Gerasimov.

A three-tiered Baroque iconostasis decorated with magnificent carving and gilding was erected before the altar in 1747. It was partially dismantled in 1853. Only the lowest tier of the iconostasis with its large eighteenth-century icons has survived.

Early twelfth-century mosaics and frescoes from the Cathedral of St. Michael of the Golden Cupolas, which are considered to be among the most outstanding art works of their era, are exhibited on the first floor in a later addition to the cathedral. Among them is the nearly intact altar mosaic *The Eucharist* and representations of the saints. The figures in St. Michael's *Eucharist* are more elongated and possess a more dynamic quality than those in St. Sophia's Cathedral. The faces of the angels and apostles are characterized by plastic strength and spirituality. The colour-range of the mosaics from the Cathedral of St. Michael is rich in green tones

and the colours are more intensive than those in St. Sophia mosaics. The contoured drawing strengthens the dramatic tension of the whole scene.

Mention should be made of a large slate relief depicting two horsemen, St. George and St. Theodore Stratelates, found on the site of the Monastery of St. Michael of the Golden Cupolas. With its flatness and rhythmic arrangement of details and figures, it is a rare example of late eleventh-century Old Russian sculpture. Kievan St. Sophia's, together with mosaics and frescoes from the Cathedral of the St. Michael of the Golden Cupolas, present the viewer with the most complete picture of artistic trends in Russia during the eleventh and twelfth centureies.

Nothing remains of the buildings that surrounded St. Sophia's in the eleventh and twelfth centu-

1699—1706 alongside the reconstruction of St. Sophia's, a large stone **Bell Tower** was built, the lowest part of which served as the main entrance to the monastery grounds. Its lush decoration makes it a striking example of early eighteenth-century Ukrainian Baroque. After a fire in 1744 the upper part of the Bell Tower was dismantled, and in 1748, two storeys, stylisticly linked with the ground floor, were added by Johann-Gottfried Schädel. In 1852, when, according to the project of the architect Paul Sparro, the third storey with its helmet-like cupola was added to it, the Bell Tower attained its current height, 76 metres.

During the years 1722—30 to the west of St. Sophia's, **a house for**

ries. After the Tatar-Mongol invasion St. Sophia's lay in ruins for a long period of time. In 1692, by decree of Peter the Great, the territory of the St. Sophia Monastery was expanded at the expense of neighbouring structures. During the years

23. Zaborovsky (West) Gate of the St. Sophia Monastery

24. Granite stele commemorating the first library in Old Russia

the **Metropolitan** was erected. It was a two-storey building with two faceted pavilions and high pediments in the central parts of the western and eastern façades. Their form corresponded with Schädel's Baroque pediment at the western gate (1746—48), the so-called **Zaborovsky Gate**, which was decorated with volutes, scalloped leaves of acanthus and mascarons and also with the crest in relief of Kiev's Metropolitan, Raphael Zaborovsky. Later, the archway of this gate was filled in. To the right of the Metropolitan's residence there is the architecturally simple Brethren's House which was constructed in the eighteenth century.

The winter single-domed refectory-type church, the so-called **Warm St. Sophia's**, was erected during the years 1722—30. It was completed in 1767 with the addition of a voluted Baroque pediment on the western façade.

On the northern side of the grounds is the elongated two-storey headquarters of the **St. Sophia Seminary** built in 1763—67 by Mikhail Yurasov. Its destinguishing features are two faceted pavilions which enliven the façade of the building, and a high mansard roof. After restoration, the building was

25. Monument to Bogdan Khmelnitsky. Detail

26. Pavilion over the Golden Gate

occupied by the Ukrainian Archive of Literature and Art.

Opposite the western façade of St. Sophia's, **a granite stele** modelled by the sculptor Ivan Kavaleridze and dedicated to the Cathedral Library was erected in 1969. On it is the low-relief representation of Yaroslav the Wise with a book in his hand and below it a quotation from the *Tale of Bygone Years*. In the centre of Bogdan Khmelnitsky Square stands a **monument to the hetman Bogdan Khmelnitsky** (*c.* 1595—1657), who led the Ukrainian people's war of national liberation against the Polish nobility, which culminated in the reunification of the Ukraine with Russia in 1654. Created after the design of the well-known Russian artist Mikhail Mikeshin, the memorial was unveiled in 1888. The dynamic figure of the horseman towers over the red granite pedestal. The monument is comparatively small, 10.85 metres high, but the successfully conceived silhouette of the sculpture and the expressive mass of the pedestal produce a sensation of majesty and strength.

The eastern side of the square is completed by an ensemble of former official buildings designed between 1854 and 1857 by the architects Mikhail Ikonnikov, Ksavery

Skarzhinsky, Ivan Strom, and others. The dryness and overloading of their façades with decorative details evidence the decline of Neoclassicism in the mid-nineteenth century.

Along the line of Yaroslav Val (Yaroslav Rampart) Street up to Vladimirskaya Street runs the old border of the ancient City of Yaroslav. In the centre of a small public garden rises a pavilion built in 1982 for the preservation of the ruins of the **Golden Gate**, which was mentioned as early as 1037 in the chronicles. Within it can be seen the remains of two walls belonging to the former tower-gate. Graffiti dating back to the eleventh or twelfth century have been discovered on the west wall. The Golden Gate was 12.46 metres high; its

27. St. Andrew's
Church

28. St. Andrew's
Church. Central
dome and vaults

passage-way, 6.4 metres wide. The pavilion contains an exhibition devoted to Old Russian architecture. At the top of Vladimirskaya Street, on the steep northern spur of Old Kiev Hill, towers one of the most amazing structures of the eighteenth century, the **Church of St. Andrew.** It was built between 1747 and 1761 according to the project of Francesco Bartolommeo Rastrelli by the architect Ivan Michurin. Its light silhouette dominates Podol and is clearly visible from the Dnieper. While working on the project, Rastrelli visited Kiev. His familiarity with the architecture of the city undoubtedly influenced the design of the church. The church is erected on a two-storey stylobate with powerful internal supports. The ovoid main dome is crowned by an onion-shaped cupola with·a cross on a golden ball. The eight windows of the tall drum harmonize with the lucarnes of the lower part of the dome. St. Andrew's is a traditional Ukrainian five-domed church, cruciform in plan, 60 metres high. The dynamic bends of the entableture, the clustered columns and pilasters with golden capitals, rounded pediments, elaborate cartouches, cascades of golden flowers and stylized shells on the green and gold background lend this church an unusual charm. A broad stairway leads to the porch and to the path surrounding the building. From here the visitor can look down on Podol, the green parks and the far reaches beyond the Dnieper.

The interior decoration of the church is a superb example of the Rococo style. The colour scheme is set by the velvety crimson ground of the tall three-tiered iconostasis, decorated with gilt carvings, sculptures and paintings. Josef Domaš, together with other masters, carved it and modelled its sculptural decor in St. Petersburg, according to a design by Rastrelli.

The Section of Painting of the Ministry for Construction, headed by the artist Ivan Vishniakov, was in charge of all the painting work for the Church of St. Andrew. In 1752, twenty-five icons and a number of sketches for the ceilings were completed by Vishniakov and his talented apprentices Alexei Belsky, Ivan Firsov, and others. The painter Alexei Antropov was sent to Kiev to mount the icons and to paint walls and ceilings. *The Lord of Sabaoth* in the centre of the dome, icons from the Feast tier of the iconostasis, the large altar composition, *The Last Supper*, and a number of other works belong to his brush. The church was finished in 1761. In 1815, the cupolas, decorated with gilt and carved alabaster, were damaged by storm. Repairs in 1828, 1867 and 1896 changed their original form. In 1963, Rastrelli's original drawings were discovered in the Albertina Museum in Vienna, which made it possible to restore St. Andrew's to its initial state during fundamental restoration in 1979.

The Church of St. Andrew stands on the site of the ancient Kiev *detinets* (Vladimir's City). Down its beautiful Andreyevsky Descent, the road leads to Podol.

Opposite the Andreyevsky Descent, Desiatinnaya (Tithe) Street leads to the park on Vladimir's Hill, where a **monument to Prince Vladimir Sviatoslavich** by Vasily Demuth-Malinovsky and Peter Klodt, sculptors, and Konstantin Thon, architect, was put up in 1853. Idealized in the manner of the Late Classicism, the bronze figure of the Prince

29. Pagan idols in Kalinin Street

30. Monument
to Prince Vladimir
Sviatoslavich

is set on a pedestal resembling a chapel of pseudo-Russian style. The silhouette of the twenty-metre monument is very expressive against a background of the Dnieper steep hills. And from the paths of Vladimir's Hill a broad view opens up on the river, the new residential areas, the parks and woodlands of the Levoberezhye (Left Bank).

At the foot of the hill where the Kreshchatic stream valley joined the Dnieper and where, according to legend, mass baptism of the Kiev population took place in the Dnieper in 988, on a pedestal, pierced by three archways, a column rises of strict Toscan order. This is a **monument to the baptism of Russia and the return of the** *Magdeburger Recht* **to Kiev.** It was built in 1802—8 according to the design of Andrei Melensky.

Not far from the monument to Vladimir Sviatoslavich, at the site of eleventh- and twelfth-century monasteries, there is a single-domed

31. Monument
to the Baptism
of Russia and
the Return of
the *Magdeburger
Recht* to Kiev

32. Refectory-type
church of
the Monastery
of St. Michael of
the Golden Cupolas

building, the former **refectory-type church of the Monastery of St. Michael of the Golden Cupolas.** This typical Ukrainian Baroque memorial, constructed in 1712 and restored in 1981 by the architect Valentina Shevchenko, became one of the branches of the St. Sophia Museum Complex of History and Architecture.

The central thoroughfare of the Upper Town, Vladimirskaya Street, connecting ancient Kiev with the newer nineteenth-century district, was built in the period of construction of **Kiev University** (1837—43) designed by Vikenty Beretti. The main features of Russian Classicism characteristic of this architect found their expression in a number of Kiev buildings and, above all, in the simple and impressive main façade of the University. The massive octastyle portico, with undecorated attic, lend an imposing note to the building.

The choice of Ionic order has aided in avoiding heaviness and squat proportions. The ensemble is completed by lateral pavilions of the Central Library of the Academy of Sciences and the University Library, which were built in 1929—30 and 1932 by the architects Vasily Osmak and Pavel Alioshin. Kiev's Taras Shevchenko University was completely reconstructed after the Great Patriotic War. A monument to the great Ukrainian poet Taras Shevchenko (1814—1861), the work of the sculptor Matvei Manizer and the architect Yevgeny Levinson, was unveiled in 1939.

Alexander Beretti, son of Vikenty Beretti, has continued the Classical tradition in the severe façade of the 1st Kiev gymnasium (now one of the University buildings), erected to his design.

On Vladimirskaya Street, between these two buildings, the Pedagogical Museum (now, the Teachers' House), one of the best examples of Neoclassicism in Kievan architecture of the early twentieth century, was built in 1909—13, according to the design of Pavel Alioshin. The half-circular central portion of its façade is an important plastic element of the surrounding ensemble. The rhythmic lines in the bas-relief frieze and the golden tone of the limestone facing lend elegance to the severe, functional form of the building.

The eclectic tendency of late nineteenth-century architecture is clearly expressed in the Kiev Opera and Ballet House, built by Victor Shreter and Vladimir Nikolayev in 1897—1901. Nearby on small Theatre Square, there is a statue of the Ukrainian composer

Nikolai Lysenko (1842—1912), the work of the sculptor Alexander Kovaliov and the architect Vasily Gnezdilov, unveiled in 1965.

Not far from Vladimirskaya Street, on Taras Shevchenko Boulevard, stands **St. Vladimir's Cathedral.** Its original design was made by Ivan Strom, and the building was begun by Alexander Beretti and Paul Sparro and completed by Vladimir Nikolayev. The construction and interior decoration took more than 30 years (1862—96). This seven-dome three-aisled church resembles the buildings of Old Russia only slightly. Its walls are overloaded with ornamental details; this spoils the wholeness of the impression.

The interior is decorated more cleverly. The marble altar screen derived from early Christian times makes for a better perception of the monumental painting.

The painting of the central nave and the chancel apse of the Ca-

thedral were executed by one of the best Russian history painters, Victor Vasnetsov (1848—1926). A large part of the work was done by the artist in 1885—96 with the help of students and teachers of the Kiev Drawing School. Together with traditional subjects of Christian iconography, Vasnetsov included portraits of many historical figures of Old Russia: Prince Vladimir Sviatoslavich (ruled 980—1015), Princess Olga (ruled 945—

33. Kiev University

34. Monument to Taras Shevchenko

964), Princes Alexander Nevsky (ruled 1252—1263), Mikhail of Tver (14th century) and the monk of Kievo-Pecherskaya Lavra, Nestor (late 11th or early 12th century). In the western part of the cathedral, to the right and left of the entrance, large compositions are painted on the walls of the nave: *The Baptism of Prince Vladimir* and *The Baptism of Rus*. Vasnetsov's interest in historical charac-

35. Pedagogical Museum (now Teachers' House)

36. Opera and Ballet House. On the right, statue of the Ukrainian composer Nikolai Lysenko

37. Cathedral of St. Vladimir

ters, costumes and the very content of the paintings show his striving to embody in his monumental works a memorial to the historical deeds of the nation.

After 1890 another outstanding Russian artist, Mikhail Nesterov (1862—1942), took part in the painting of the cathedral, mainly contributing large compositions in the choir gallery and icons for the altar screen of the north and south chapels.

Very original decorations on the arches and walls of the cathedral belong to Mikhail Vrubel's brush (1856—1910).

In spite of the eclecticism felt in all the cathedral's decoration, this memorial is one of the more significant and characteristic examples of monumental art of the second half and end of the nineteenth century.

Art Museums.
Kreshchatik

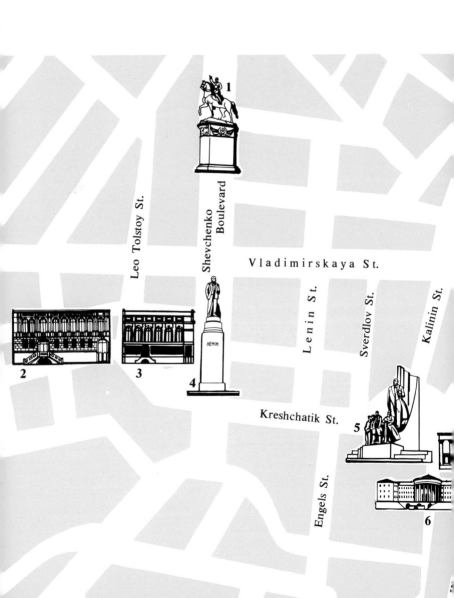

Leo Tolstoy St.

Shevchenko Boulevard

Vladimirskaya St.

Lenin St.

Sverdlov St.

Kalinin St.

ЛЕНІН

Kreshchatik St.

Engels St.

2

3

4

5

6

1 Equestrian statue of Nikolai Shchors
2 Museum of Western and Oriental Art
3 Museum of Russian Art
4 Monument of Lenin
5 Monument to the October Revolution
6 October Palace of Culture
7 Museum of Ukrainian Art
8 Branch of the Central Lenin Museum
9 Monument dedicated to the re-union of Russia and the Ukraine

Geroyev Revolutsii St.

8

Vladimirsky Descent

9

Naberezhnoye Highway

The Dnieper

The Dnieper

On its way to Kreshchatik, Taras Shevchenko Boulevard crosses Repin Street, where there are two museums, one of Russian art, the other of Western and Oriental art, and where a statue of the great Russian artist Ilya Repin was unveiled in 1984.

The Kiev Museum of Russian Art (founded in 1922) has one of the largest collections of works of art by Russian artists, ranging from the twelfth century to our day. It was based on the collection of the Tereshchenko family of industrialists and other private collections. Severe in form, the building of the museum was erected in 1882—84 by Andrei Gun and Vladimir Nikolayev. The interior was designed by Robert Friedrich Meltzer, known for his work in the Winter Palace in St. Petersburg and for the construction of a number of exhibition pavilions.

The exhibits are arranged in thirty-five rooms in the three storeys of the building. The most ancient work in the section of Old Russian art of the twelfth to seventeenth centuries is the large icon of *Sts. Boris and Gleb*, the first canonized Russian saints and the young sons of Vladimir Sviatoslavich. The icon was found in a Novgorod

monastery, but its monumental style, notwithstanding later over-painting, indicates its affinity with the Kiev art school of the twelfth and early thirteenth centuries. The exhibition also displays many first-class examples of icon painting of the Novgorod, Rostov-Suzdal and Moscow schools. Among them two late fifteenth-century icons of the Feast tier are supposedly from Kargopol — *The Last Supper* and *The Beheading of John the Baptist*. The sonorous colour scheme is characteristic of the sixteenth-century icons of the Deesis and Feast tiers which are close in manner to icons done by painters of the Dionysius circle.

Russian art of the eighteenth century is excellently represented by its portrait painting. Dmitry Levitsky, one of the most poetic of the artists of the latter half of the eighteenth century, reveals the delicate charm of the epoch in his portraits of an unknown woman in blue (1784) and of the writer Ivan Dol-

gorukov (1782). Among the large collection of portraits of another great master of late eighteenth and early nineteenth centuries, Vasily Borovikovsky, with their strict compositional structure and inner nobility, the portrait of Vera Arsenyeva (1795) attracts our special attention.

The relatively small collection of paintings and sculptures of the first half and mid-nineteenth century is characterized by a skillful selection of works. *The Portrait of Maria Pototskaya, Her Sister Sophia Shuvalova and the Ten-year-old Ethiopian Girl* (1835—36), painted in a romantic vein, is one of the most charming efforts of Orest Kiprensky. The works of Vasily Tropinin, a former serf, are well represented. Romantic and realistic tendencies are combined in the portraits of Prince Alexander Meshchersky (1849) and Semion Likhonin (1841) by Karl Briullov. Alexander Ivanov's study *Head of the Trembling One* for his *Appearance of Christ to the People* is exceedingly dramatic.

The display of mid-nineteenth-century art is rounded off with the small but tragic picture *The Gamblers* (1852) by Pavel Fedotov, the leading artist of the so-called natural school.

The endeavours of Russian painters of the latter half of the nineteenth century are displayed more abundantly. This is above all the works of Nikolai Gay, executed at different periods of his activity.

Here are exhibited the sunny landscapes of Italy, the artist's last self-portrait (1892—93), and a few of his last expressive studies produced for the unfinished painting *Calvary* (1893).

The canvas of Vasily Perov, *God's Fool* (1875—79), showing a lone figure in the snow, is outstanding in its spontaneous vitality. Ivan Kramskoi, the theorist of the democratic trend in Russian art and prominent artist, occupies a large place in the display. His *Contemplator* (1876) awoke great interest in Fiodor Dostoyevsky. The artist's *Peasant with a Bridle* (1883), full of inner tension, should also be noticed. The genre painting of Vladimir Makovsky *Peasant Girls' Party* (1882), cap-

41. *Self-portrait*
by Nikolai Gay

42. *Portrait of
an Unknown Lady
in Blue* by Dmitry
Levitsky

43. *Gamblers*
by Pavel Fedotov

turing the wedding customs of the Ukraine, is always popular with viewers, as is the dramatic picture of old prerevolutionary life *No, you won't!* (1892). Nikolai Yaroshenko in one of his best work, *Girl Student* (1883), shows us a poetic yet prim image of one of the representatives of progressive youth of the 1870s and '80s. Also on display is the unique collection of masterful landscapes by Ivan Shishkin and sculptures by Mark Antokolsky.

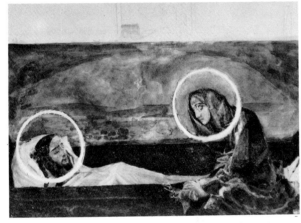

44. *Three Tsarevnas
of the Underground
Kingdom*
by Victor Vasnetsov

45. *The Lamentation*
by Mikhail Vrubel.
Sketch for a painting
in St. Vladimir's
Cathedral
(not realized)

The paintings by Ilya Repin in the museum show only certain sides of this talented Russian artist's work. On display is the *Head of a Peasant* (study for the *Religious Procession in Kursk Province*, 1880—83), the dramatic image of Gogol's character in *Notes of a Mad Man*, Poprishchin (1882), and the painting *St. Nicholas of Myra Delivers the Three Innocent Men* (1889), in which persons sentenced to death are depicted with moving sincerity. The brightly coloured canvas of Victor Vasnetsov, *Three Tsarevnas of the Underground Kingdom* (1884), on a theme from a Russian fairy-tale is among the more significant and characteristic of his works.

In the same hall we find works by the famous history painter Vasily Surikov, paintings and poetic landscapes by Vasily Polenov, Apollinary Vasnetsov and Isaac Levitan.

A separate room is provided for the studies and paintings of Vasily

Vereshchagin. His large canvas *The Conquerors* (1878—79) is one of the most powerful anti-war pictures ever painted. It was the result of the artist's emotional reaction to his service with the army during the Russo-Turkish War of 1877—78.

Ivan Aivazovsky, the famous Russian marine painter, is also well represented in the museum with highly distinctive pictures in his special field.

Paintings collected by the museum fully illustrate the leading trends in Russian art of the late nineteenth and early twentieth centuries. The spiritual and creative quests of the artists at the turn of the century are reflected by Mikhail Nesterov. (See *On the Hills*, 1896, and the studies and sketches produced for the painting *Old Russia*).

Mikhail Vrubel occupies a special place it the art of this period. The depth of his insight, the emotional intensity and the splendid painting technique captivate the viewer of the canvas *Girl with a Persian Rug in the Background* (1886) and studies and sketches for unconsummated paintings of the Vladimir Cathedral.

Attention should also be given to individual paintings by Valentin Serov, Konstantin Korovin, Victor Borisov-Musatov, Nikolai Roerich, Boris Kustodiev, and Zinaida Serebriakova, sculptures by Pavel Trubetskoi, Anna Golubkina, Sergei Konionkov, and other artists,

46. *On the Hills* by Mikhail Nesterov

47. *Students of the Workers' Faculty* by Boris Ioganson

all of them members of the most important art groups of the early twentieth century, such as World of Art, Union of Russian Artists, and Jack of Diamonds.

Soviet artists of the 1920s and '30s reflected the revolutionary events in the life of the country and created images of the heroes building the new socialist society. The bright colour scheme together with truthfulness in expressing the characters of young workers, to whom the road to knowledge was now open, attract the viewer to Boris Ioganson's *Students of the Workers' Faculty* (1928). Serafima Riangina's *Higher and Higher* (1934) shows the spiritual uplift and optimism of the builders of the first five-year plans. A tendency to monumentality is noted in such Alexander Deineka's works as *Girl Student* (1938), *Runner* (1939) and *Encounter with Beauty* (1960).

A prominent place in the art of the 1940s was won by the *Collective-farm Threshing-floor* (1949) by Arkady Plastov. Rooms devoted to Soviet art genre pictures and graphics also contain works by Pimenov; portraits by Igor Grabar, Martiros Saryan, Sergei Gerasimov, Georgy Riazhsky and Fiodor Bogorodsky; landscapes and still lifes by Piotr Konchalovsky, Ilya Mashkov, Robert Falk, Alexander Kuprin, Georgy Nissky and Nikolai Romadin; sculptural pieces by Nikolai Andreyev, Ivan Shadr and Yekaterina Belashova.

48. *Katerina* by Taras Shevchenko. The Taras Shevchenko Museum

Soviet art of the 1960s and '70s is represented by Gely Korzhev, Victor Ivanov, Vladimir Stozharov, Leonid Kabachek, the Tkachiov brothers, and others.

The exhibition of the museum is rounded off by the small though carefully selected articles of Russian and Soviet decorative applied art. Attention may be directed to the superb specimens produced at Russian porcelain factories in the eighteenth to twentieth centuries, especially to statuettes and Soviet propaganda porcelain of the 1920s and '30s, and to the wooden articles painted at the folk workshops of Palekh and Khokhloma, etc.

The Museum of Western and Oriental Art, founded in 1919, was built by Robert Friedrich Meltzer

49. Museum
of Western
and Oriental Art

50. Hall of Italian
Art

51. *Sts. Sergius
and Bachus*

52. *The Adoration of the Magi* by the Master of the Khanenko Adoration of the Magi

53. Budhisattva

54. *Portrait of the Infanta Margarita* by Diego Velazquez

in the 1880s. It occupies a mansion resembling an Italian palazzo of the sixteenth century. The collection of the well-known Kiev archaeologist Bogdan Khanenko and his wife formed the nucleus of the museum. Now the museum's collection is considerably enlarged. Many of its exhibits, for instance the early Byzantine icons and paintings of the Chinese Middle Ages (fourteenth to nineteenth centuries), deservedly have attracted worldwide interest.

Ancient art is displayed in a hall on the ground floor and contains a rich collection of Corinthian and Attic painted vases from the fourth and third centuries B.C., which were found in archaeological digs of the ancient towns of the Northern Black Sea coastlands. In addition, the visitor will find here rare examples of polychrome Etruscan statuettes (400 B.C.) and Roman sculptural portraits of the second century A.D.

The European Middle Ages are represented by items produced by Italian masters of the fourteenth to sixteenth centuries, including the most complete collection in the world of sixth- and seventh-century Byzantine encaustic icons, early fourteenth-century unique reliquaries and paintings by Barnaba da Modena (*Scenes from the Life of Christ*. 1350—1400) and the Master of the Osservanza (*The Crucifixion*. Mid-15th century).

Jacopo del Sellaio, a master famous for his paintings on *cassoni*, whose style is similar in its elegance to Sandro Botticelli's, is represented by a complicated dramatic composition which is illustrating the poetic world of *Orpheus and Euridice* (latter half of the fifteenth century).

The Madonna and Child of Pietro Perugino, the teacher of Raphael, is embued with a quiet harmony, while another *Madonna and Child* captivates with its expressive power; it belongs to the brush of Giovanni Bellini, the first master of the High Renaissance of the Venetian school in the late fifteenth and early sixteenth centuries. This collection is supplemented by a polychrome stucco cast of the *Madonna and Child* of the eminent fifteenth-century Italian sculptor Donatello and by a rich collection of fifteenth- and sixteenth-century Italian majolica. Italian painting of the seventeenth and eighteenth centuries is repre-

55. Equestrian statue of Nikolai Shchors

56. Statue of Lenin

sented by pictures of Luca Giordano, Alessandro Magnasco, Giovanni Battista Tiepolo and by a romantic view of Venice by Francesco Guardi (*Canal in Venice*. 18th century).

The next hall is devoted to the art of Spain and France of the seventeenth and eighteenth centuries. Diego Velazquez's *Portrait of the Infanta Margarita* (late 1650s), painted from the life, charms with its noble grandeur and sonorous colour scheme. The canvas was a study for a large formal portrait, now housed in the Prado, Madrid. Next to Velazquez's canvas is a small exquisite *Still Life with a Chocolate-grinder* (1640), the work of another Spanish artist Francisco Zurbaran and his son Juan. In this same hall pictures by prominent French

painters of the eighteenth century are hung: François Boucher, Louis Tocqué, Jean-Baptiste Greuze and a picture by Jacques Louis David, a celebrated painter of classic subjects, *Portrait of Lazare Hoche* (1793).

English painting of the eighteenth century is represented in the museum by the canvas of Joshua Reynolds *Rogue* (1780s).

The room where objects illustrating the applied art of eighteenth-century France are displayed is decorated with Brussels tapestries on the theme of *Don Quixote* (1720s) in the Rococo style.

The museum has a small but well-selected collection of old Netherlandish paintings and a number of works by prominent artists from Flanders and Holland of the seventeenth century. The diptych *Ado-*

ration of the Magi, the work of an anonymous artist of the late fifteenth century, has won a wide and well-deserved fame. This artist was close to the circle of Hugo van der Goes, and in the early twentieth century he was called the Master of the Khanenko Adoration of the Magi.

The Flemish school of painting at the peak of its development is represented by a number of works, including a forcefully executed sketch for an allegorical composition by Peter Paul Rubens (1610—1620s), a canvas by Jacob Jordaens *Pleasant Dream* on the theme of *Cupid and Psyche*, realistic genre compositions by David Teniers the Younger, and a lyrical *Winter Scene* by Gijsbrecht Leytens (?).

Among seventeenth-century Dutch paintings are *A River Scene* by Jacob van Ruisdael, genre paintings by Dirck Hals and Jan Steen and some canvases which were executed by artists of the Rembrandt circle.

A large number of exhibits is devoted to ancient and medieval China. Here the visitor will find ancient bronzes, potteries and polychrome wooden figures of the seventh to sixteenth centuries, ceramics, porcelain and ivories of the eighteenth and nineteenth centuries, and Chinese paintings of the Ming (1368—1644) and Ch'ing (1644—1912) dynasties.

57. Kreshchatik

Works of Chinese artists of the second generation of Southern Sung (twelfth and thirteenth centuries), Ma Yüan (*Visit to the Waterfall*) and Hsia Kue, are presented in copies and variations by fourteenth- to sixteenth-century masters. A large part of the collection is devoted to portraits of the Ming Dynasty and to works executed by artists of the Ch'an philosophical sect, who exerted great influence upon the culture and art of Japan.

The museum displays an interesting collection of items of Japanese applied art and of woodcuts of the Ukiyo-e school (eighteenth and early nineteenth centuries).

58. October Revolution Square

59. Monument to the October Revolution. Detail

Ancient wooden sculptures of India, unique thirteenth- to seventeenth-century illuminations and miniatures, the work of Arabian, Mesopotamian, Persian and Central Asiatic masters, are also well represented.

A collection of Egyptian sculpture of 3000—1000 B.C. and of fifth- to seventh-century Coptic fabrics is on view on the second floor. The head of an Egyptian noble of mid-3000 B.C. is one of the best sculptures produced in the Old Kingdom to be found in Soviet museums. A splendid relic of the New Kingdom is the figure of the God Thoth, made of black basalt in the form of a sitting baboon (mid-2000 B.C.). A small statue of kneeling Nesnebneteru, the ambassador of Queen Amenardes, relates to the period of the Ethiopian dynasty (6000 B.C.).

The art of Mongolia and Tibet is represented by Tibet icons and small ritual figures.

Worth noting too are objects illustrating the arts and crafts of the Peoples of Asia — eighth- to thirteenth-century ceramics unearthed on the site of Afrasiab, an ancient town in Central Asia, metal work from Central Asian Soviet republics and the Caucasus, rugs and carpets from Turkmenia and Azerbaijan.

The Taras Shevchenko Museum is situated at the junction of Taras Shevchenko Boulevard and Repin Street. Here the visitor will find the most complete collection of the paintings and drawings of the great Ukrainian poet and artist and also many works of his Russian and Ukrainian contemporaries, among them a portrait by Karl Briullov of the poet Vasily Zhukovsky. The young Taras Shevchenko was bought from serfdom in 1838 with the money this portrait brought in a lottery.

An equestrian statue of the hero of the Civil War, Nikolai Shchors (1895—1919), was unveiled in 1954 at the junction of Taras Shevchenko Boulevard and Comintern Street which leads to the Kiev Railway Station. The granite pedestal, on which the bronze statue of the Soviet commander is placed, is decorated with a bronze bas-relief frieze depicting Civil War episodes. The monument is the work of the sculptors Mikhail Lysenko, Nikolai Sukhodolov, Vasily

Borodai, and the architects Alexander Vlasov and Alexei Zavarov. **A statue of Lenin** (1946) on a square paved with granite slabs at the head of Shevchenko Boulevard is carved from polished red labradorite by the well-known Soviet scupltor Sergei Merkurov and mounted on a granite pedestal which was designed by the architects Alexander Vlasov and Victor Yelizarov.

On Bessarabian Square, opposite Shevchenko Boulevard, stands a monumental building housing Kiev's first indoor market, an example of the Art Nouveau architecture of the early twentieth century, designed by Heinrich Gay in 1910 — 12. The square and boulevard command a fine view of Kiev's central thoroughfare, **Kreshchatik.** The Kreshchatik ensemble, destroyed by the Nazi invaders in 1941—43, was built anew after the Great Patriotic War. Only a few structures typical of early twentieth-century architecture were restored to their original aspect. They included the former bank buildings (No 32, put up in 1913 by Friedrich Johann Lidval; No 8a, built in 1911 by Leonty Benois, and No 8b, erected in 1913 by Pavel Andreyev).

The width of modern Kreshchatik is 75—100 metres. Architects made a successful use of the hilly relief, designing edifices with various silhouettes and volumes. A maze of streets connects Kreshchatik with the Upper Town, Pechersk and Podol. Three squares — Leninsky Komsomol, October Revolution and Bessarabian — are linked with the main thoroughfare.

60. October Palace of Culture

61. Ante-room in the Branch
of the Central Lenin Museum

62. Branch of the Central Lenin Museum

Oktiabrskoi Revolutsii (October Revolution) Square is not only the compositional centre of the ensemble but also its historical centre. Here the road from the Liadskiye Gate to Pechersk passed through. The place is associated with heroic episodes in the defense of the city against the Tatar-Mongol hordes in 1240. Strong fortifications were built here with wooden towers and gates by Russian armies defending Kiev from the Turkish intervention at the end of the seventeenth century. In 1737—40, in their place the stone Pecherskiye Gate was erected, which remained until 1833. This monument of ancient architecture was excavated by archaeologists in 1981, and a fragment of it is on display in the underground passage under the square. The present-day square resembles an amphitheatre. On the upper terrace of the stairway leading to Hotel Moskva (designed by Boris Priymak and others), **a monument to the October Revolution** was unveiled in 1977. It consists of a massive pylon, 18.4 metres high, symbolizing a banner on which the figure of Lenin is silhouetted, carved in red granite. Before and below the pylon, four bronze figures stand: a worker, a woman worker, a sailor and a soldier — fighters for the Revolution. The monument is the joint work of the sculptors Vasily Borodai and Valentin and Ivan Znoba and the architects Alexei Malinovsky and Nikolai Skibitsky.

On a high hill in the green of chestnut trees, we see the **October Palace of Culture,** formerly the Boarding-school for Young Ladies of Noble Birth, built by Vikenty Beretti in 1839—42 in the style of Neoclassicism. It was restored in 1952—57.

A simple cubic form of the **Kiev Branch of the Central Museum of Lenin,** built by Vadim Gopkalo, Vadim Grechina and others in 1982, lends Leninsky Komsomol Square its severe appearance. The Dnieper Hotel, built by Victor Yelizarov and Natalia Chmutina in 1956—64, on the other side of the square, completes this architectural ensemble.

From Leninsky Komsomol Square, a broad stairway leads to Pioneer Park, which is part of an enormous green belt stretching on high Dnieper terraces toward the Kievo-Pecherskaya Lavra.

Amidst the green stands the **monument commemorating the 325th anniversary of the reunion of Russia and the Ukraine,** designed by Alexander Skoblikov, sculptor, and Igor Ivanov and Konstantin Sidorov, architects. It is a composition consisting of an arch with figures of an Ukrainian and a Russian and a bas-relief on the theme of Russo-Ukrainian brotherhood.

The Museum of Ukrainian Art is situated on Kirov Street. It was built by Vladislav Gorodetsky as Kiev's first City Museum of Antiquities and Art, according to a design by Boitsov. The sculptural dec-

63. Monument dedicated to the reunion of Russia and the Ukraine

oration was by Elio Salya. The high-relief composition in the tympanum of the pediment symbolizes the triumph of the arts. The museum was opened in 1899. From the very first day, along with the archaeological and historical sections, the section of fine arts was created. In 1936, the historical section withdrew to an independent organization, and the Museum of Ukrainian Art was formed. The large collection of paintings, drawings and sculptures embraces all periods of the development of Ukrainian fine arts and is arranged in twenty-one rooms.

The oldest exhibit displayed in the museum is the wooden polychrome relief of *St. George with Scenes from His Life* produced in the twelfth or thirteenth century. The image of the young warrior in a golden suit of armour with a purple cloak in style and character is very similar to works of Byzantine masters.

Also of interest is the fourteenth-century icon of the *Virgin Hodegetria*, from the town of Lutsk in Volhynia.

The end of the sixteenth and the early seventeenth centuries were marked by the establishment of a narrative tendency in icon painting. The desire of the artist to show what he saw in his visual environ-

64. Museum
of Ukrainian Art

65. Hall of Ukrainian
Soviet Painting

66. *Sts. Barbara and
Catherine*

67. *Portrait
of Dmitry Dolgoruky*
by Master Samuel

ment — the specific features of everyday life and costume — was quite evident. Dramatic scenes depicted in some icons reflect the events of the people's fight against the Polish and Lithuanian invaders. The early seventeenth-century icon *Passions* is a memorial of these times.

In the latter half of the seventeenth century, after the Ukraine was united with Russia, the interest of artists in life around them gave their paintings a secular inclination. Among numerous icons of the late seventeenth and early eighteenth centuries which showed secular influence are the following: *The Intercession* (late seventeenth century), which contains a portrait of the hetman Bogdan Khmelnitsky; *The Crucifixion* showing the picturesque figure of the commander Leonty Svechka dressed in a long-skirted red jerkin (late seventeenth century); and *St. Barbara and St. Catherine* (first half of the eighteenth century) in brocaded court costumes.

Late Baroque art (mid-eighteenth century) is represented by icons of the Deesis tier from the iconostasis of the Church of the Resurrec-

eighteenth century. The naive style of this monument reminds us of eighteenth- and nineteenth-century Ukrainian folk art. This art is represented by a number of pictures varying the image of the Ukrainian Cossack. The pictures are accompanied by long rhymes or even prose in the Rabelaisian style of seminarist interludes. This indicates their connection with the Ukrainian national theatre and with its popular hero, not without his comic aspects, the Zaporozhye Cossack.

The art of the late eighteenth century definitely broke with icon-painting traditions of the past. The

tion in the village of Berezna in the vicinity of Chernigov (1760s). In the next room, we find the largest collection of Ukrainian portrait art, folk art and wooden polychrome figurines. The formal portraits of Cossack commanders are extraordinarily effective.

Attention should be given to the portrait of the young monk Prince Dmitry Dolgoruky (1769) by the prominent Kievan painter Samuel who skilfully emphasized the sitter's chaste dignity.

In the centre of the room is a painted wooden statue, *Samson and the Lion*, which used to decorate the fountain on former Kontraktovaya Square in Podol in the early

sily Borovikovsky, painted in St. Petersburg at the end of the eighteenth century. Academy graduates came from St. Petersburg to Kiev bringing new professional skills and aesthetic principles.

The trends toward realism and romanticism assumed a leading place in Ukrainian painting and graphics in the first half and middle of the nineteenth century. The museum displays Vasily Tropinin's portraits of peasants clearly demonstrating these trends. A lofty romantic attitude to people and to his native land is characteristic of the paintings and drawings of Taras Shevchenko. His last *Self-portrait* (1861) is especially em-

68. *Girl from Podolia* by Vasily Tropinin

69. *On a Moonlight Night* by Konstantin Trutovsky

static conventional pose disappeared from portrait painting. This is evident from even a casual comparison of the formal portraits of Cossack commanders with the works of Dmitry Levitsky and Va-

bued with dramatic undertones. The poetry of old homesteads and national costumes, the beauty of the Ukrainian landscape, and somewhat sentimental scenes of everyday life have found their place

70. *The Cossack Mamai Playing a Pandora*

in paintings, watercolours and sketches from nature by Shevchenko's contemporaries and followers, such as Vasily Sternberg, Ivan Sokolov, Lev Zhemchuzhnikov, Konstantin Trutovsky, and others.

Realistic traditions of genre painting were developed by artists of the latter half of the nineteenth century, which were closely bound to the ideals of the Itinerants (Society for Travelling Art Exhibitions) including Nikolai Pimonenko, Kiriak Kostandi and Nikolai Kuznetsov. Famous Ukrainian genre paintings, *Wedding in Kiev Province* (1891), *At the Well. Rivals* (1909) and a dramatic scene from provincial life of the country, *Victim of Fanaticism* (1899), by Pimonenko were very popular even outside the Ukraine. In contrast to the narrative character of the canvases mentioned above the paintings of Alexander Murashko, the most important Ukrainian artist of the turn of the century, are distinguished by extraordinary expressive power. A student of Ilya Repin, Murashko felt the influence of Sezession and other trends of Western European art. His portraits and paintings of various periods are on display in the museum.

Landscape painting has an important place in the exhibition. Here we may see the lyrical canvases of Sergei Svetoslavsky, the works of Sergei Vasilkovsky, Ivan Trush and Nikolai Burachek.

The Art of the Soviet Ukraine section is opened by the laconic posters of the revolutionary years, sketches for revolutionary propaganda decoration, works by leading graphic artists of the first decade after the October Revolution. Among them are the elegant sheets of Georgy Narbut, sketches for panels and paintings by Vasily Yermilov, the famous poster of Adolf Strakhov *V. Ulyanov (Lenin)* (1924), expressive drawings by Sophia Nalepinskaya-Boychuk

71. *Liquidating Illiteracy* by Vasily Sedliar

72. *Conquerors of Wrangel* by Fiodor Krichevsky

and prints by Vasily Kasiyan, all of them imbued with the severe romance of the revolutionary epoch.

The museum's collection of Ukrainian paintings and graphics of the 1920s is the most complete one in the Soviet Union.

Here, too, are shown the powerfully expressive paintings of Anatoly Petritsky and the monumental works of Timofei Boychuk, Vasily Sedliar and Ivan Padalka.

Fiodor Krichevsky, who has taught several generations of contempo-rary painters, such as Tatyana Yablonskaya and Georgy Melikhov, is represented by a large number of paintings. His triptych *Life* (1925—27) and the large-scale intensely colourful canvas *Conquerors of Wrangel* (1934) have occupied an important place in the development of realistic painting in the Soviet Ukraine.

Ukrainian art trends of the 1930s and '40s are represented by Alexei Shovkunenko's masterly water-colours, landscapes and portraits, Karp Trokhimentko's canvas

73. *Father and Son*
by Tatyana
Yablonskaya

Workers of Dnieprostroi, Nikolai Samokish's fierce battle scenes (*The Battle of Maxim Krivonos with Jeremy Vishnevetsky*, and others), Pavel Volokidin's portraits and by the paintings of the younger generation of painters, Fiodor Klichko, Mikhail Ivanov and Alexei Nesterenko.

Feats of the people in the struggle against Nazism and for a peaceful life became the main themes of artists in the post-war years. These themes are interpreted in the paintings of Vladimir Kostetsky (*Return*. 1947) and Victor Puzyrkov (*Black Sea Sailors*. 1947), in the canvases of Tatyana Yablonskaya, Georgy Melikhov, Sergei Grigoryev and Nikolai Glushchenko.

The pictures by artists from the Soviet Trans-Carpathians, Josif Bokshai, Andrei Kotska, Fiodor Manailo and Gavriil Gliuk, attract with the originality of their images and intensity of their colour scheme. A large number of exhibits are by young painters, graphic artists and sculptors, who came forward with their new artistic ideals in the 1960s and '70s.

Visiting the museum the art lover may trace the progress of Ukrainian art during the 700 years of its existence.

Pechersk.Vydubichi

1 Mariinsky Palace
2 Monument to Ivan Franko
3 Monument to General Nikolai Vatutin
4 Monument to the Insurgent Arsenal Workers
5 Bust of Alexander Pushkin
6 Monument to the founders of Kiev
7 Vydubichi Monastery
8 Moscow Upper Gate
9 Askold's Tomb
10 Park of Eternal Glory
11 Ukrainian Museum of the History of the Great Patriotic War (1941—45)

Kirov Street, one of the main thoroughfares of old Pechersk, runs along a broad parkland which is spreading out over the high Dnieper terraces. Not far from Leninsky Komsomol Square, at the junction with Petrovsky Avenue, a monument to Grigory Petrovsky (1878—1958), a Soviet statesman, was inaugurated in 1970. It is the work of the sculptor Alexei Oleinik and the architect Igor Lanko. Opposite it is the Dynamo stadium, where a monument by Ivan Gorovoi to the Kiev football players who were shot by the Nazis in 1941 was erected in 1971.

This part of Pechersk was built up in the mid-eighteenth century. In 1750—55, a palace was erected above the steep slopes to the Dnieper, which came to be called the **Mariinsky Palace**. It was designed by Ivan Michurin, Andrei Kvasov and Piotr Neyolov. This light elegant structure in the Baroque style, with its broad half-circular windows, white paired half-columns against turquoise walls and a high parapet with a balustrade decorated with fanciful vases, was to a great extent a copy of Francesco Bartolommeo Rastrelli's building in the village of Perovo near Moscow. The front court with modest

one-storey pavilions on each side, opens onto the small Sovetskaya (Soviet) Square, with an observation ground affording a fine view of the Dnieper in the distance. The north side of the palace with a stairway terrace seems to merge into the luxuriant greenery of the park, laid out according to Rastrelli's design. The upper wooden floor of the central portion of the palace burned in 1819 was rebuilt in the 1870s, in stone, by Karl Mayevsky.

Another stone building of the mid-eighteenth century, the **Klovsky Palace**, designed by Johann-Gott-fried Schädel and Piotr Neyolov, was constructed in 1752—56 on the southwest side of the Pechersk plateau. It was a simple two-storey building; a third floor was added later, in 1863. At present the Klovsky Palace houses the Museum of the History of Kiev.

In the early nineteenth century, there was a shady linden grove between the Klovsky and Mariinsky Palaces, giving the name *Lipki* (Ukrainian for linden-trees) to the whole district. On the old estate, a small house has survived belonging to the family of General Nikolai Rayevsky, a hero of the War of

74. Supreme Soviet of the Ukrainian SSR and the Mariinsky Palace

75. Monument to General Nikolai Vatutin

76. North façade of
the Mariinsky Palace

77. Klovsky Palace
(now Museum of
the History of Kiev)

1812. The great Russian poet Alexander Pushkin (1799—1837) visited this house in 1821. The future participants of the Decembrist Uprising in St. Petersburg in 1825 also gathered here.

In this part of Kirov Street there are small buildings from the turn of the century as well as contemporary monumental structures, among which the solid edifice of the **Council of Ministers of the Ukrain-**

ian **SSR,** erected in 1935—37 to the design of Ivan Fomin and Pavel Abrosimov, is particularly striking. On the park side of the street is the **Supreme Soviet of the Ukrainian SSR**, built in 1936—39 by Vladimir Zabolotny. The Mariinsky Palace and the Supreme Soviet building overlook the Sovetsky (Soviet) Park containing monuments to heroes of the October Revolution (1927, designed by Vasily Onashchenko; reconstructed in 1949) and to the participants of the January armed uprising of 1918 in Kiev (the first 1927 monument was demolished; the present-day memorial by Vasily Vinaykin, sculptor, and Vasily Gnezdilov, architect, was unveiled in 1967; relief on the pedestal by Vladimir Klimov used to decorate the 1927 monument).

79. Council of Ministers of the Ukrainian SSR

78. Memorial to the Insurgent Arsenal Workers

In the central area of the park towers the **monument to the hero of the Great Patriotic War, liberator of Kiev, the Hero of the Soviet Union, General Nikolai Vatutin,** the work of the sculptor Yevgeny Vuchetich and the architect Yakov Belopolsky. The statue, carved out of grey granite and mounted on a four-faceted pedestal, stands out clearly against the green park landscape. It was unveiled in 1948.

At the beginning of Yanvarskogo Vosstaniya (January Uprising) Street are seen the towers of the former St. Nicholas barracks with St. Nicholas's Gate (1846—50) built in medieval castle style. Opposite it, we see the walls of the

legendary Arsenal Plant, criss-crossed with machine-gun bullets and shrapnel from the time of the revolutionary battles of 1917—18. A relief on the wall commemorating these events is by Nikolai Kovtun and Maria Korotkevich. It was fixed on the wall in 1961. This group of buildings forms an architectural ensemble of Geroi Arsenala (Heroes of the Arsenal Plant) Square, in the centre of which rises a **memorial to the insurgent Arsenal workers** — a piece of field artillery on a pedestal of granite blocks — unveiled in 1923. The mansion of Ypsilanti has been declared an architectural monument; it was built in 1798 for the

80. Palace of Young Pioneers and Schoolchildren

81. Monument to Ivan Franko

82. Bust of Alexander Pushkin

commandant of the Pecherskaya fortress. From 1807—16 Konstantinos Ypsilanti (1760—1816), Count of Moldova and Walachia, participant of the Greek anti-Turkish freedom movement, lived there. The house was restored in 1981—82.

At the junction of present-day Yanvarskogo Vosstaniya Street and Suvorov Street a bronze **bust of Alexander Pushkin** was unveiled in 1899. It was cast after the model of Robert Bach in order to commemorate the centenary of the poet's birth.

A picturesque Dnieper terrace before Slava (Glory) Square is occupied by the ensemble of the **Palace of Young Pioneers and Schoolchildren** built in 1965 by Abram Miletsky and Eduard Bilsky, with the participation of the artists Ada Rybachuk and Vladimir Melnichenko and the sculptor Vasily Bo-

rodai. The interior of the light-filled building of glass and concrete is decorated with mosaic panels, reliefs and ceramics. All buildings comprising the ensemble are excellently blending with the surrounding area.

From the square by the Dnieper descent we may pass to **Askold's Tomb.** According to legend, Kiev's ruler Askold was cravenly killed in 882 by the Novgorod ruler Oleg. Here in 1810 a small classical church-rotunda was built by Andrei Melinsky. In 1936, a collonade was added to it, according to the design of Piotr Yurchenko.

The square in front of the Palace of Young Pioneers and Schoolchildren provides a fine view of the **Park of Eternal Glory.** A straight avenue bordered by pollarded hornbeams leads to the **graves of**

heroes of the Great Patriotic War (1941—45). In the centre of the tomb of the Unknown Soldier, on a bural mound faced with granite, is the Eternal Flame and a black obelisk. This memorial, the work of Abram Miletsky, Vladimir Baklanov, Vladimir Novikov and Ivan Pershudchev, was unveiled in 1957.

Close to the Park are the ramparts of the Old Pecherskaya Fortress. Raised in 1679, they enclosed the territory of the ancient village of Berestovo and the Kievo-Pecherskaya Lavra.

The ancient Russian chronicles often mentioned Berestovo, the favourite country residence of the founder of the Kievan state, Vladimir Sviatoslavich and his successors. Here between 1113 and 1125 Vladimir Monomachus built a stone Church of the Transfiguration of Our Saviour, in which his younger son, Yuri Dolgoruky (1125—1157), the founder of Moscow, was buried. Of the ancient three-aisled church only the narthex remained, to which later the chancel was added. The thickened *nervures* (ribs) of the vault and the lancet-shaped windows make this building the only monument in Kiev which retains the architectural traits of Late Gothic. In 1642—44, the church was painted by skilled Greek masters from Athos together with Kiev icon-painters. During restoration work in 1970, large fragments of frescoes of the first half of the twelfth century were cleaned

83. Memorial in the Park of Eternal Glory

in the western part of the church, including a large-scale composition (4.4 by 2.7 metres), *Christ Appearing to His Disciples at the Sea of Tiberias*. In spite of the poor state of preservation of the paint layer, the figures and the head of the Apostle Peter testify to the great skill of ancient artists. The seventeenth-century painting was transferred by the restorers to a new base.

South of the Church of the Transfiguration of Our Saviour, at Berestovo, is located the monastery ensemble, **Kievo-Pecherskaya Lavra**. It was created over a period of nine centuries. In the eleventh and twelfth centuries, it was constructed by unknown builders of Kievan Rus, and in the seventeenth to nineteenth centuries by Russian and Ukrainian architects, artists and masters of decorative and applied arts.

---

84. Askold's Tomb

The Pechersky Monastery was founded, according to the chronicles, by the monk Antony, a native of Liubech in the Chernigov area, and his follower Theodosius in 1051. In the beginning the monks used the caves for cells, and the future name of the monastery, Pechersky, was derived from the Old Slavonic word meaning a cave. As time went on, the territory of the monastery gradually expanded. In the years of the rule of Prince Iziaslav, a large low hill near the village of Berestovo was given to it. There, in 1073, the monastery's Father Superior Theodosius laid the foundation of the Cathedral of the Dormition. Since that time the territory of the monastery has been divided into two sections: the **Upper Lavra** (on the hill) and the **Lower Lavra,** together with the **Nearer and Farther Caves.**

In the twelfth century, the Upper Lavra continued to expand. Stone gates were raised with the Trinity

Gatechurch on them, and at the end of the twelfth century, stone walls were added. The Pecherskaya Lavra became an important cultural centre in Old Rus. Here the main chronicles were written: at the turn of the twelfth century, the famous Nestor-chronicler created splendid examples of Old Russian literature, *The Tales of Bygone Years* and *The Life of St. Theodosius*. Moreover, in the Kievo-Pecherskaya Lavra, builders and artists were trained. History has preserved the name of the famous late eleventh- or early twelfth-century master Alimpy, who headed the icon-painting workshop. With the icon-painters of his circle, we associate several old icons, for instance, *The Virgin Great Panagia* (about 1114) from the Tretyakov Gallery, Moscow. The Tatar-Mongol invasion severely damaged the Pecherskaya Lavra. Stone walls were razed, church interiors were destroyed, many valuables and genuine works of art were looted.

The first attempts to rehabilitate the buildings came in the latter half of the fifteenth century. In 1470—71, under that last Kiev Prince, Simeon Olelkovich, the Cathedral of the Dormition was rebuilt. The art of this period is represented by small polychrome reliefs, at present mounted in the walls of the Lavra's Great Bell Tower under the arches of the first tier.

After the unification of the Ukraine with Russia (1654), construction was undertaken on an unprecedented scale. In 1698—1701, the territory of the Upper Lavra was provided with stone walls and three observation towers — Ivan Kushchnik, Maliarnaya and Clock Towers. Under the walls under-

85. Church of
the Transfiguration
of Our Saviour
in Berestovo

86. Detail of
a seventeenth-century
fresco

87. Detail of
a twelfth-century
fresco

89. View of the Upper Lavra

88. Map of the Kievo-Pecherskaya Lavra

1 Gatechurch of the Trinity
2 Church of St. Nicholas of the Infirmaries
3—4 Former monks' dormitories
5 Great Bell Tower
6 Ruins of the Dormition Cathedral
7 Economic Block
8 Church of All Saints on the Economic Gate
9 Church of the Transfiguration of Our Saviour in Berestovo
10 Kovnir building (now the Ukrainian Museum of Historical Treasures)
11 Printing-house (now the Ukrainian Museum of Books and Printing)

12 Metropolitan's house (now the Museum of Ukrainian Folk Decorative Art)
13 Refectory with a church
14 Observation ground
15 Tower-like Church of St. Humphrey
16 Clock Tower
17 Ivan Kushchnik Tower
18 Bell Tower at the Nearer Caves
19 Church of the Exaltation of the Cross at the Nearer Caves
20 Church of the Nativity of the Virgin
21 Kovnir Bell Tower

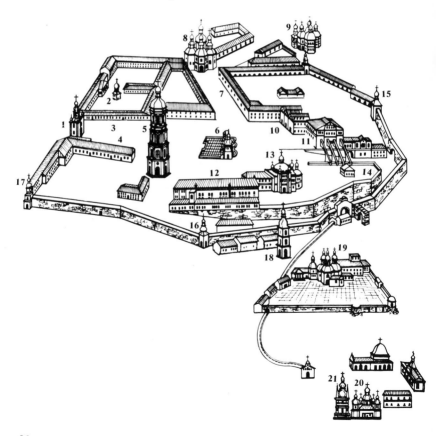

ground passages were dug, *slukhi*. The work was supervised by the master Dmitry Aksamitov. Three churches — the Trinity Gate-church, the tower-like Church of St. Humphrey and the Church of All Saints built by an unknown Kiev architect on the Economic Gate — were incorporated in the system of fortification.

In 1718, a raging fire destroyed all wooden structures of the Lavra and damaged the interiors of the stone churches. A new period of construction in the Kievo-Pecher-skaya Lavra began in 1720 and continued well into the latter half of the eighteenth century. The ensemble took on an external aspect that has to a large extent persisted to the present. The scope of building in the Lavra from the 1720s to '40s may only be compared to the construction in St. Petersburg.

By decree of Peter the Great, the architect Fiodor Vasilyev was sent to Kiev with a team of experienced builders. Johann-Gottfried Schädel, worked at the Lavra from 1731 to the end of his days. A number of talented local masters also took part in this work: the builder Stephen Kovnir, the expert masters of carving Vasily Stefano-

90. Kievo-Pecherskaya Lavra. Gatechurch of the Trinity with monks' dormitories on either side

91. Gatechurch of the Trinity. Interior

92. Gatechurch of the Trinity. Iconostasis

vich (who decorated the façades of the Trinity Church) and Grigory Petrov (who created the great iconostasis of the Dormition Cathedral), jewellers, and gold- and silversmiths, such as Ivan Ravich, Mikhail Yurevich, Samson Strelbitsky, and many more.

Construction in the Lavra continued in the nineteenth and early twentieth century. In 1926, the Kievo-Pecherskaya Lavra and the Church of the Transfiguration of Our Saviour in Berestovo were declared a state museum of history and culture.

The Nazi invasion caused considerable damage to the museum. In the immediate post-war years

intensive work on rebuilding and restoring was started.

The main entrance to the museum territory is from Yanvarskogo Vosstaniya Street. Opposite the museum is the Arsenal, an old, solid building which is constructed in the style of Russian Classicism (1784—98).

Beyond the Arsenal a silhouette of the Church of St. Theodosius of the Caves (1698—1702), an example of Ukrainian Baroque, is seen. **The Trinity Gatechurch** dates back to the twelfth century. Built between 1106 and 1108, it was part of the original fortifications. This is the starting-point of our tour through the Upper Lavra.

The Trinity Church is a small one-domed four-pillar construction

93. *The Virgin Orans*

94. *Youth in a Chariot Drawn by Lions*

with a cruiciform plan and three apses. Only the south wall has preserved the laconic forms of twelfth-century Russian architecture. In the 1830s, the east and west sides were decorated with undulating pediments, pilasters, luxuriant floral ornaments and cartouches with paintings and gilt. The cupola form was also changed and a narthex in the Baroque style was added on the north. The interior of the church was painted in tempera in 1734—44.

The compositions, crowded with figures, remind us of Ukrainian icons and portraits of this period. In the architectural and landscape backgrounds there is a real sense of depth, but a three-dimensional representation of space is combined with a flat treatment of the draperies and luxurious attire, which strengthens the decorative effect of the interior painting. The compositions reflect the influence of the secular art of eighteenth-century Western European engravings. Notice especially the *Baptism of an Ethiopian* occupying the north wall and the *Nicene Council* on the west wall, which are treated in a manner contemporary to the artist. In the individuals surrounding the Emperor Constantine and the bishops, we can see the

96. Relief by Ivan Martos from the tomb of Field Marshal Piotr Rumiantsev-Zadunaisky from the Dormition Cathedral

95. Tomb of Prince Konstantin Ostrozhsky from the Dormition Cathedral. Detail

faces of real persons. Two compositions representing the procession of the righteous stand out in their beautiful colouring and free execution, the one on the vault and the other over the entrance in the central section of the church. Here we sense the hand of a master well versed in the Italian school of painting.

The Trinity Gatechurch was painted by the best local masters: Feoktist Pavlovsky, Ioann Maximovich, Alimpy Galik, and many others. The carved and gilded iconostasis installed about 1730 is exceptionally effective. At this time the floor of the church was covered

97

with iron plates cast at Demidov's works in the Urals.

From the main gates of the Lavra there is a fine view over the central square and **ruins of the Dormition Cathedral** (eleventh to nineteenth centuries), which was blown up by the Nazi invaders in 1941. The absence of the powerful and expressive silhouette of the cathedral, so familiar from photographs and drawings, is especially felt. It contributed a sense of wholeness and nobility to the surrounding buildings, erected in various times. And even now the ruins of its walls are impressive. Distinctly visible is the foundation of the central part, the oldest part of the eleventh-century great three-aisled single-domed structure with three faceted altar apses. Byzantian architects spent six years on the construction and decoration of this magnificent cathedral.

97. Chasuble. Detail

98. Chasuble

99. Mitre

100. Great Bell Tower and ruins of the Dormition Cathedral

101. Museum
of Ukrainian Folk
Decorative Art (former
Metropolitan's houses)

Stone monks' dormitories were built in the eighteenth century on either side of the main gates. In these buildings an exhibition has been arranged of applied art of the seventeenth to nineteenth centuries and of engravings by well-known Lavra artists of the late seventeenth and eighteenth centuries, Leonty and Alexander Tarasevich, Innokenty Shchirsky, Grigory Levitsky, and others. In the sec-

102. *Visiting the Lion* by Maria Primachenko

103. *Good Time* by Hanna Sobachko-Shostak

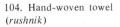

104. Hand-woven towel
(*rushnik*)

105. Candelabrum

106. Vessel in
the form of a lion

107. Ukrainian Museum of Books and Printing (former printing-house)

108. Engraving by Gregory Levitsky in the *Encomium of Zaborovsky*

tion devoted to the history of the architectural ensemble of the Kievo-Pecherskaya Lavra photographs and a model of the Dormition Cathedral are on display, as well as some items of its interior decoration dated from the eleventh to nineteenth centuries. Among them are two unique eleventh-century slate reliefs showing Samson (or Hercules) rending open the jaws of a lion, and a youth in a chariot drawn by lions. Judging by their size, these slate reliefs used to decorate the enclosure of the choir gallery in the Dormition Cathedral.

Among the other sculptural works which decorated the interior of the cathedral was the tomb of Prince Konstantin Ostrozhsky. Created in 1579, it was destroyed in 1941. Its copy is now on view. There is also a marble relief (1805) from the tomb of the Russian Field Marshall Piotr Rumiantsev-Zadunaisky (1725—1796), which was executed by the famous sculptor Ivan Martos.

The main architectural feature, setting the tone to the ensemble of the Kievo-Pecherskaya Lavra, is the **Great Bell Tower** built in 1731—44 by Johann-Gottfried Schädel. The four-tiered structure, 96.5 metres high, is the greatest achievement of the architect. Its dimensions are proportional to the mass of the cathedral, while the strict rhythm of the columns dividing the walls of each tier provide a noble restraint and classical severity to the whole aspect of the bell tower. In building the cornices and capitals, large ceramic units were used, which was a progres-

sive step in architectural practice of that time. The bells weighing 6,000 *poods* (about 100 tons) were installed on the third tier; a large clock was put up on the fourth tier. The present clock, made in Moscow, was mounted in 1903. Its mechanism was connected to a system of seven bells, of which the oldest had been cast in 1743 by the Tula master Andrei Maliarov.

109. Double-page spread of the *Fasting of St. Basil the Great*

110. *St. John Chrysostom's Homilies.* Title page and its detal

Next to the Great Bell Tower, a small house for the Lavra governor was built by Schädel.

On the south side of the central square there are two eighteenth-century **Metropolitan's houses** with an adjoining private church (1904—5), where since 1954 the **Museum of Ukrainian Folk Decorative Art** has been located. Here more than 50,000 exhibits have been gathered.

Unusually rich is the collection of rugs and carpets, eighteenth- and nineteenth-century fabrics and embroidery, wood carvings and other types of handicrafts. Here, too, are works by prominent folk painters, Hanna Sobachko-Shostak, Paraska Vlasenko, Maria Primachenko and Yekaterina Belokur; articles produced at faience and porcelain factories; objects of art glass, including examples of free-blown *huta* glass. Next to the Metropolitan's houses is the Refectory with a church built by Vladimir Nikolayev in 1893—95. The church is in plan a square and is covered with a spherical dome, twenty metres in diameter. It has an architectural

111. Ukrainian Museum of Historical Treasures (former Kovnir building)

112. Sword (*akinaka*)

113. Shoulder bands (*bramy*)

prototype, the Cathedral of St. Sophia in Constantinople. Its interior decoration was designed by Alexei Shusev, and the walls were painted by Lavra masters under the supervision of Ivan Izhakevich.

The Ukrainian historical figures, Ivan Iskra and Vasily Kochubei, executed in 1708 by the hetman Ivan Mazepa, are buried by the walls of the Refectory. They are all mentioned in Alexander Pushkin's narrative poem *Poltava*.

An observation ground provides a fine view of the Nearer and Farther Caves.

On the east of the central square the old printing-house (1701—73) stands, which houses the **Ukrainian Museum of Books and Printing.** Here also is one of the most interesting public structures — the so-called **Kovnir building** which combined the bakery and the book store and is decorated with six tall pediments. The walls of the ba-

kery were erected in the seventeenth century, but its modern aspect the building received in 1744—46, when it was rebuilt after a fire by the building master Stephen Kovnir. In 1969, the house was given over to the **Ukrainian Museum of Historical Treasures** with its exceptionally rich collec-

114. Church of All Saints on the Economic Gate

115. Church of St. Nicholas of the Infirmaries

tion of golden articles from various periods of history, including the treasures from the Gaimanov grave and Tolstaya grave, gigantic Scythian burial mounds dating back to the fourth century B.C. On display is the burial of a Scythian queen with her child from the Tolstaya grave. Among the treasures found in this burial mound are a gold sheath of a short sword (*akinaka*) decorated with reliefs, openwork masks, golden plaques and pendants, and a splendid relic of antique jeweller's skill, a massive gold pectoral (breast ornament) with scenes of Scythian everyday life and mythological motifs (fourth century B.C.). Special attention may be drawn to articles from the burial mounds of Sarmatian queens (100 B.C. to the first and second centuries A.D.) made by Egyptian, Greek, Persian and Indian craftsmen. Massive gold personal ornaments inset with pearls and precious stones from the rich treasure found near the village of Glodosa in Kirovograd district (fourth to the early eighth centuries) are also on display. The great skills of Kievan jewellers are demonstrated by golden shoulder bands (*barmy*), temple pendants, a diadem unearthed in the village of Sakhnovka, and other articles executed in the elaborate technique of *cloisonné*.

The museum possesses many articles by Russian and Ukrainian gold- and silversmiths of the fourteenth to sixteenth centuries. These include icon and gospel mounts set with emeralds, rubies, sapphires and pearls; mitres and chalices. Among the highlights of the collection are objects of jewellery made by Kievan masters Ivan Ravich, Ivan Moshchenko, Mefody Narbutovich, and others.

Worth noting is the numismatic section containing a superb collection of coins and medals.

To the north of the central square, the group of so-called Economic buildings is located. Along the two-storey Economic Block, the street leads to the Economic Gate, with the **Church of All Saints** (1696—98) over it. The church is one of the most complete architectural

examples of late seventeenth-century Ukrainian Baroque. Cruciform in plan, it has a tower-like silhouette, four faceted apses with lanterns and slender drums with golden helmet-shaped cupolas topped by shining crosses. An open arcade on low columns in front of the main entrance to the church was built in the first half of the eighteenth century. The existing wall paintings were done at the beginning of the twentieth century by a team of artists under the supervision of Ivan Izhakevich. In type they follow the tradition of the realistic art of Victor Vasnetsov and the decorativeness characteristic of Mikhail Vrubel.

To the north of the Trinity Gate-church is the **monastery of St. Nicholas of the Infirmaries,** founded in the twelfth century, with a small seventeenth-century church. Behind it, in a two-storey building is the **Ukrainian Museum of Theatre, Cinema and Music,** founded in 1926. The rich collection of this museum contains costumes, stage sets, drawings and photographs embracing the century-old history of folk and professional theatre in the Ukraine, from the seventeenth and eighteenth centuries to our day.

From the central square the road descends under the powerful buttresses which support the walls of the printing-house down to the South Gate, leading to the Lower Lavra. It was built in the early nineteenth century by Andrei Me-

lensky in Classical style. Opposite it, the covered way to the Nearer Caves begins.

The cave monastery of the Lower Lavra and St. Sophia's Cathedral alike are the oldest and most famous sites in Kiev. Eighteenth- and nineteenth-century surface buildings at the Nearer Caves are unpretentious and expressive. The small **Church of the Exaltation of the Cross** with three apses, facing south, east and west, was built in ·1700. The 1769 Baroque iconostasis is the work of the wood carver Karp Shverin. Icons placed on it

belong to the eighteenth century. The surviving paintings of the interior were done in the late nineteenth century.

The two-tier **Bell Tower** (1763—68) located on the slope of the hill, unites the architectural ensemble of the Upper Lavra with that of the Farther Caves.

Recent excavations have shown that the passageways in the Nearer Caves are more than half a kilometre long. Many grafitti in Church Slavonic, Polish and Armenian languages were found on their walls.

116. View of the Lower Lavra

111

117. Church
of the Exaltation
of the Cross at the
Nearer Caves

118. Old Russian
necropolis
in the Nearer Caves

119. Iconostasis
of the Church of
the Exaltation
of the Cross

The galleries of the Nearer Caves on the walls of which are fragments of eighteenth-century paintings lead to three underground churches: St. Antony's, St. Barlaam's and the Church of the Presentation of the Holy Virgin. These churches' vaults rest on marble columns taken from the Dormition Cathedral's altar screen dismantled in the seventeenth century. Their present-day gilded copper iconostases were made by Kievan goldsmiths in 1813—19, and the floors were covered with iron plates produced at the Tula works as early as the eighteenth century. The Nearer Caves have a special historical value as the burial place

of Kievan Rus, whose history extends back into the un-chronicled past. A number of religious and political figures is buried there — Antony, the founder of the monastery, Nikon, called the Great, the author of the first chronicle record, Nestor, the author of the *Tale of Bygone Years,* Alimpy and Grigory, the first Old Russian iconpainters, the healers Agapit and

120. Church of the Nativity of the Virgin and the arcades at the Farther Caves

121. Bell Tower at the Farther Caves

122. Moscow Upper Gate at the Pecherskaya Fortress

114

Damian, and the authors of the most ancient part of the Kievo-Pechersky Patericon (*Lives of the Church Fathers*), Simon and Polikarp.

A covered gallery connects the Nearer Caves with the Farther Caves. The underground passageways of the Farther Caves are 280 metres long. Of the three twelfth-century cave churches, the Church of the Nativity of the Virgin, the Church of the Annunciation, and St. Theodosius's Church, the latter is the largest. Its four-tier copper iconostasis, decorated with relief

work, was executed in the eighteenth century.

The group of buildings delightfully situated on a high green hill, over the Farther Caves, was constructed in the seventeenth and eighteenth centuries. They lend a sense of wholeness to the architectural ensemble of the Farther Caves. Among these buildings is the Church of the Conception of St. Anne, built in 1679. Owing to later alterations it lost its original aspect. Opposite it stands the seven-domed Church of the Nativity of the Virgin (1656). Its corner chapels were added to the main building in the eighteenth century. A breast-wall with a staircase and a range of arcades carried on double piers was erected at its base also in the eighteenth or in the early nineteenth century.

The ensemble is completed by the two-tiered **Kovnir Bell Tower,** 40

metres high, amazingly elegant and
original. The decorative features
of Ukrainian Baroque blend with
the rich and forceful architectural
design which shows the impact of
the Rastrelli school. Some investi-
gators consider this edifice to be
the project of Ivan Grigorovich-
Barsky. The construction of the
Bell Tower lasted from 1754 to
1761, with the participation of the
Lavra masters Stephen Kovnir and
Semion nicknamed the Italian.

123. Ukrainian Museum of the History
of the Great Patriotic War (1941—45)

124. Monument to the founders of Kiev

The latter is responsible for the ornamental motifs which are decorating its walls.

Close to the territory of the Farther Caves the sightviewer can see the massive ramparts of the Old Pecherskaya Fortress, with the stone **Moscow Upper Gate** (1765). This is one of the few well-preserved examples of secular architecture of the mid-eighteenth century. From here there is a fine view of the magnificent memorial, **the Ukrainian Museum of the History of the Great Patriotic War of 1941—45,** founded in 1981. The plan of the memorial was conceived by the sculptor Yevgeny Vuchetich and the architect Yevgeny Stamo. The work was accomplished by a large team of architects, engineers and sculptors of Moscow and Kiev under the supervision of Victor Yelizarov, architect, and the sculptors Vasily Borodai, Friedrich Sogoyan, and others.

The broad path with stairways leads to a concrete tunnel which is decorated with five bronze high-relief compositions devoted to the feats of Soviet soldiers at the front and workers for the war effort in the rear. On the main square are two bronze sculptural groups, of 100 figures, 4 to 4.5 metres high.

The museum building is crowned with a stainless-steel figure, 62 metres high, of a woman symbolizing the Motherland. A sword and shield in her hands embody the concept of defence of the motherland. The total height of the monument is 102 metres. The exhibition halls are decorated with mosaic panels, paintings and sculptures by Soviet artists. Opposite the monument, on a tall cliff above the bank of the Dnieper, is the bowl of the Eternal

Flame of Glory. The broad avenue devoted to hero-cities is lined with granite blocks. The memorial, built in the park named after Yevgeny Vuchetich, towers above the square of the Heroes of the Great Patriotic War and Druzhby Narodov Boulevard.

At the foot of the high terraces of the Pechersky plateau, near the Dnieper, in the Primakov Park, a monument was unveiled in 1982 to the founders of Kiev, the brothers Kiy, Shchek and Khoriv and their sister Lybed. It is the work of the sculptor Vasily Borodai and the architect Nikolai Feshchenko.

125. View of the Vydubichi Monastery

Lower downstream on the Dnieper, between the Navadnitskaya valley and the mouth of the Lybed River on Zverinetskaya Hill, stretches an ancient woodland, the hunting grounds of Old Kiev's princes, now the territory of the Botanical Gardens of the Ukrainian SSR Academy of Sciences. The hills towering above the Dnieper were called Vydubichi. The name is probably derived from the Ukrainian word meaning 'to be washed up' (*vydubal*). An old legend tells how an idol of the pagan god Perun, thrown into the Dnieper after the acceptance of Christianity, was washed up on the sand bar at their foot. Here Prince Vsevolod, the younger son of Yaroslav the Wise, erected his fortified palace, Red Court, in the eleventh century. Closer to the bank of the river, he built the splendid three-aisled **Church of St. Michael** (1070—88). This was the earliest building of the **Vydubichi Monastery.** To guard the church from the swift waters of the Dnieper, which nibble at the bank, the architect Piotr Miloneg designed a system of breast walls in 1199—1200. They stood fast more than 300 years, till the beginning of the sixteenth century, when the eroded riverbank fell in together with part of the church. The remaining west side of St. Michael's was used by the builders when they began to erect a new church in the early seventeenth century. Its contemporary aspect this small single-domed church attained after the renovation undertaken by Mikhail Yurasov in 1770—75. A fragment of the eleventh- or twelfth-century fresco, *The Last Judgement*, gives us an idea of the original interior decoration of St. Michael's. The free and forcefully executed figure of an angel was found under layers of eighteenth- or early nineteenth-century overpainting during restoration in 1968.

The second period of stone construction in the Vydubichi Monastery occured in the late seventeenth and eighteenth centuries. At this time outstanding examples of Ukrainian Baroque were constructed here — the well-balanced **St. George's Cathedral** (1696—1701), **the refectory-type Church of Our Saviour** with wall paintings dating from the eighteenth and nineteenth centuries and the solid three-tiered **Bell Tower** (1727—33). The five-domed St. George's

126. Cathedral of St. George

127. Church
of St. Michael

Cathedral consists of five faceted tower-like sections forming in plan a cross. In its external aspect — walls decorated with pilasters, columns and cartouches — it is very similar to the Church of All Saints on the Economic Gate in the Kievo-Pecherskaya Lavra. Evidently, both constructions were created in the late seventeenth or in the first third of the eighteenth century by the same architect, whose name has not come down to us.

The buildings of the Vydubichi Monastery nestle beautifully among the hilly relief. They complete the architectural ensemble on the Kievan heights on the south as does the Church of St. Andrew on the north.

Podol. Kureniovka. Obolon

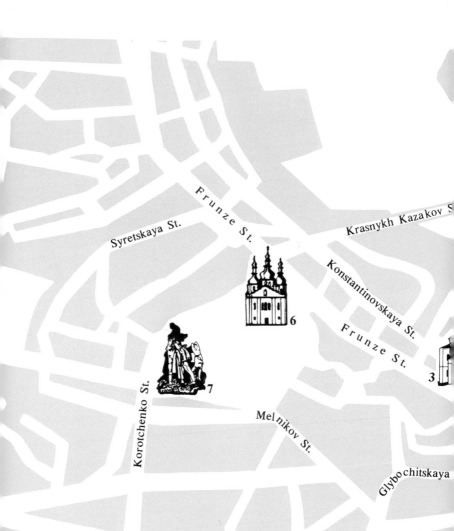

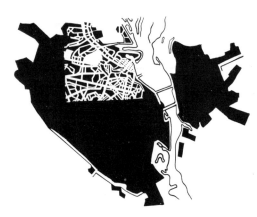

The Dnieper

1   Statue of Grigory Skovoroda
2   House of Contracts
3   Residence of Peter the Great
4   Church of the Intercession
5   The Samson fountain
6   Church of St. Cyril
7   Memorial to Soviet citizens,
    soldiers and officers killed by the
    Nazis at Baby Yar

Elektrikov St.

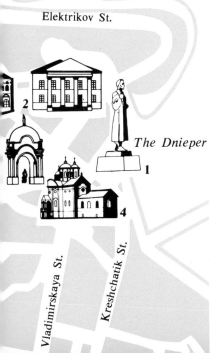

The Dnieper

Vladimirskaya St.

Kreshchatik St.

The present-day Vladimirsky Descent to Podol passes by Vladimirsky Hill. It connects Leninsky Komsomol Square with Pochtovaya (Post-office) Square, where the single-storey post-office building is preserved. Opposite it, on the Dnieper Embankment, is the river-boat station.

The road connecting Podol with the Pecherskaya Fortress was built in the eighteenth century and was considerably improved and widened in the early nineteenth century. Not far from Pochtovaya Square, on Zhdanov Street, several houses dating back to the late eighteenth and early nineteenth century have survived (Nos. 20, 27a and 27b).

The lowland occupied by Podol is bounded on the south and on the west by three hills, Starokievskaya, Zamkovaya and Shchekavitskaya. In Kievan Rus Podol was separated from the Dnieper by the Pochaina River (now Pochaininskaya Street), at the mouth of which was a harbour. Judging from archaeological excavations, in the tenth to twelfth centuries, Podol was built up with wooden houses located near the harbour and marketplace. Hundreds of ships from Constantinople, Italy and

countries of the Arabian East dropped anchor at this harbour.

In 945, the first wooden Church of St. Elias was built near the harbour. In 1692, on its site was constructed the stone **Church of St. Elias.**

The Podol districts were inhabited by very different social classes. Rich estates of the tenth and eleventh centuries with two- or three-storey castle-like houses surrounded by oak fences with observation towers at the corners, were excavated on present-day Red Square. On the slopes of the ravines, on the banks of the streams and small rivers that ran into the Pochaina, the craftsmen lived in small wooden houses. The old names of the ravines indicate that

128. Gateway
to the Church
of St. Elias

129. The former
Kievo-
Mogilianskaya
Academy

130. House of
the goldsmith
Strelbitsky
(now Museum of
the History of Podol)
and the Church
of the Intercession

126

they settled in communities — Gonchar (potters), Kozhemyak (leather workers). In addition, jewellery, leather and glass workshops were discovered during excavations. In the eleventh to thirteenth centuries, the wooden buildings lining the streets alternated with the stone cathedrals mentioned in the literature and known from archaeological data. For instance, not far from today's Red Square, there was a stone Church of the Virgin in Pirogoshchi (1132—36), mentioned in the famous poetic epic of Old Rus, *The Lay of Igor's Host.* As is well known it was similar to the Cathedral of the Dormition in the Kievo-Pecherskaya Lavra.

In the fourteenth and fifteenth centuries, after the Tatar-Mongol invasion, when the Upper Town lay in ruins, Podol became the central region of Kiev. However, in the period of Lithuanian and Polish rule right up to the reunification of the Ukraine with Russia in 1654, stone construction in Podol practically stopped.

The oldest architectural monument of Podol is the small single-storey **Church of St. Nicholas Pritisk,** built in 1631.

In the late seventeenth and early eighteenth centuries, buildings of the Bratsky Monastery were grouped around the central square of Podol. They included the stone Church of the Epiphany, the building of the **Kievo-Mogilianskaya Academy,** which was turned into the Academy of Free Sciences in 1701, and the Town Hall, graced with a tower and a spire. At present, only the Academy has survived **(now the Branch of the Central Library of the Academy of Sciences of the Ukrainian SSR).** It was rebuilt in 1732—40 by Johann-Gottfried Schädel. To the ground floor with a massive arcade resting on columns, Schädel added an upper storey with a colonnade and small church in a corner part of the structure. In the courtyard of the Academy, a sun dial was installed in the late eighteenth century in the form of a column on a tetrahedral base.

In the late seventeenth and in the eighteenth century, the Kiev Academy was the largest educational institution not only in the Ukraine but in Russia. At various times many illustrious persons have studied within its walls: the composer Dmitry Bortniansky, the great Russian scholar and poet Mikhail Lomonosov, the Ukrainian philosopher Grigory Skovoroda, the Kievan architect Ivan Grigorovich-Barsky to name but a few. In 1977, **a statue of Grigory Sko-**

131. Statue of Grigory
Skovoroda and the
House of Contracts

132. Residence
of Peter the Great

133. Church
of St. Cyril

134. Altar screen
of the Church
of St. Cyril

voroda by Ivan Kavaleridze was unveiled on Red Square.

One of the oldest secular buildings in Kiev is the two-storey house at the corner of Konstantinovskaya and Khoriv Streets. Built at the end of the seventeenth century, it was the **residence of Peter the Great** when he lived in Kiev in 1706—7. This building, situated not far from the seventeenth-century fortified ramparts (now Verkhny Val and Nizhny Val Streets), combines the features of a dwelling house and fort. An open arcade of the first storey was built on the massive stone porch in the 1740s.

A number of Podol buildings were designed by Ivan Grigorovich-Barsky in the second half of the eighteenth century. His **Church of the Intercession of the Virgin** (1766) is an elegant example of Late Baroque. An open rotunda with a high dome, also his creation, was raised over the **Samson fountain** in Podol's main square in 1748—49 (in 1981, it was restored to its original aspect).

The rectangular **Gostiny Dvor** (shopping arcades) in the centre of Red Square was built in 1809 according to the plan of the well-known architect Luigi Rusca. After the fire of 1811 that destroyed most of Podol, the building was reconstructed by Andrei Melensky. In the early ninetenth century, the court architect William Hastie designed a new building plan for this district: quite wide streets for this time were to intersect at right angles; in the centre was to be Kontraktovaya (Contract) Square (now Red Square) with the Town Hall and the **House of Contracts.** However, this plan, confirmed in St. Petersburg, did not take into account the local relief. The project was begun with some small changes in 1812. The Town Hall was not built, and only the House of Contracts, rectangular in plan, with its Doric portals on the façades, gives us an idea of Hastie's project, which was conceived in the classical style.

Among architectural ensembles built in Podol in the style of Neo-classicism in the first third of the nineteenth century, we should note the constructions by Andrei Melensky on the territory of the St. Florus Convent. Their focal point is the Church of the Resurrection (1824), surrounded by an elegant Ionic colonnade.

Beyond the Verkhny Val and Nizhny Val Streets is a plain called Ploskaya (flat). At the foot of picturesque hills ran the north road which was leading to Vyshgorod — Kirillovskaya Street (now Frunze Street).

On high terraces and at their foot, archaeological excavations have unearthed Stone and Bronze Age sites and numerous remains of settlements and temples of Old Rus. Not far from Kirillovskiye heights,

135. *An Angel
Rolling
up the Scroll of
the Heavens*

136. *St. Cyril of
Alexandria Writing
a Homily*

137. *Descent of
the Holy Spirit*
by Mikhail Vrubel

at the junction of the roads leading to Chernigov, Novgorod and Vladimir Volynsky, the village of Dorogozhichi (Dorozhichi) was situated. At this place in 980 the host of Vladimir Sviatoslavich was encamped, preparing for battle for the Grand Prince's throne with Vladimir's brother Yaropolk.

On a high hill over Dorogozhichi, the pretender to the Kievan throne, the Chernigov Prince Vsevolod Olgovich, erected his castle and founded a small monastery. After his death in 1146, his widow built a small stone **church** in the monastery in hononur of **St. Cyril of Alexandria**. It was three-aisled and single-domed with the external walls decorated with *zakomaras*. In the eastern section, the naves

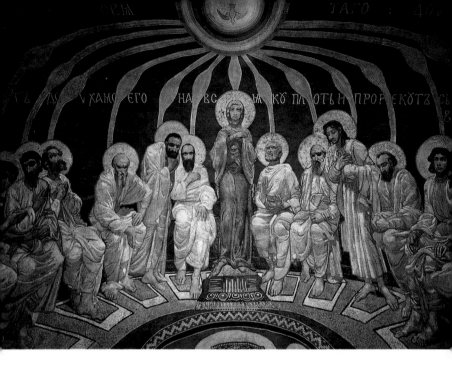

are finished with semicircular altar apses. A narrow band of blind arcading in the upper parts of the walls and the drum and other constructive features of the building lead to the conclusion that it was designed by Chernigov architects. The church was painted in the mid-twelfth century. More than 800 square metres of frescoes have survived to the present day. The surviving paintings are, for the most part, fragments of large-scale compositions. *An Angel Rolling up the Scroll of the Heavens,* one of the most interesting fragments, is, for instance, part of the *Last Judgement.*

In spite of certain traditional motifs in the interior decoration, in the paintings of St. Cyril's Church there are many new features, and many subjects have never been encountered before.

In the large many-figured compositions, such as the *Nativity of Christ* and the *Dormition of the Virgin,* Christian symbolism is blended with an abundance of everyday-life details. In the cycle of frescoes in the south apse, the ascetic figure of St. Cyril is opposed to the lively individual characters surrounding him. Some stylistic features characteristic of the frescoes show a bond with the Balkan artistic school. The images of Macedonian saints in the north apse confirm this suggestion.

The frescoes in St. Cyril's Church were painted by several artists. Even a casual comparison of the elegant style of the *Presentation of Christ in the Temple* and *An Angel Leading Young John the Baptist into the Wilderness* with the naive but forceful monumentality of *The Apostle Paul, Emperor Constantine and Empress Helen* reveals differences in technique. After the Tatar-Mongol invasion the monastery was abandoned. In the course of the following centuries, the St. Cyril Church was rebuilt several times. In the eighteenth century, it differed radically from the original building. In place of the old dome five new ones were built, and the western façade was embellished with a Baroque pediment. In 1884, Mikhail Vrubel, as yet a little-known artist, was invited from St. Petersburg to aid in the restorational work, which was supervised by Professor Adrian Prakhov. The artist executed the monumental compositions still decorating a marble altar-screen of the church, which held a notable

place in the treasury of Russian art of the nineteenth century. These are *The Descent of the Holy Spirit, Angels with Labarums, The Archangel Gabriel* (in the scene of

The Annunciation), *The Lamentation*. Attention may be also directed to his icons, *The Virgin and Child, Christ, St. Cyril* and *St. Aphanasius*.

In 1929, the Church of St. Cyril was converted into a history museum. During the 1960s and '70s, the surviving eleventh-century frescoes were cleaned and Vrubel's compositions, painted in oil on walls and vaults, were restored. At the end of the nineteenth century, the place where this ancient church is located was a remote borderland, called Kureniovka, surrounded by meadows, sloping to the banks of the Dnieper. The Baby Yar ravines cut deep into the plateau. In the period of Kiev's occupation by the Nazis, their slopes were red with blood: for more than a hundred thousand Soviet citizens were brutally killed here. In 1976, in memory of this tragic event, in the park between Korotchenko, Dorogozhitskaya and Melnikova Streets, **a memorial** was unveiled **dedicated to the Soviet citizens, soldiers and officers, prisoners of war, who were tortured and killed by the Nazi invaders in 1941—43.** It was the work of Mikhail Lysenko, Victor Sukhenko and Alexander Vitrik, sculptors, and Nikolai Ivanchenko, Anatoly Ignashchenko and Victor Ivanchenkov, architects.

138, 139. Memorial to Soviet citizens soldiers and officers, prisoners of war, brutally killed by the Nazis at Baby Yar in 1941—43

140. Obolon housing estate

135

To the north of Baby Yar, along Frunze and Vyshgorodskaya Streets, there was a district of old suburban villages. Now this region is one of beautiful new housing estates, Vetrianye Hills (1961—65) and Vinogradar (begun in 1973), with high-rise buildings, large shopping centres, movies and schools.

The new housing blocks surrounding Shevchenko Square grew up in a picturesque place called "Kin grust" (Throw off your troubles). Beyond the new district stretches one of the largest woodland parks, Pushcha-Voditsa, covering an area of more than thirty thousand hectares. In Kievan Rus the dense forest was the hunting preserve of the Princes. Today the park has about forty sanatoriums and rest homes for Kiev's citizens.

The newest and biggest housing estate of Kiev is Obolon, in a region where archaeologists have discovered ancient settlements from the beginning of our era. In the pagan period the temple of the god Veres, patron of cattle, was situated here. Obolon was often mentioned in the chronicles as the field where the nomads who attacked Kiev were met in battle. Later the flood-meadows of the lower Dnieper valley served as haymaking and pasture land for local people. Construction of housing on silted land began in 1968. The combination of high-rise houses and the low buildings of shopping centres and schools creates a con-

trasting architecturally expressive silhouette, interesting to view from across the Dnieper. The housing units with their parks and manmade lakes have definitely improved the microclimate of Obolon. Circular roads connect the streets with the main highway and with Moscow Bridge across the Dnieper built in 1976 by the architect Vladimir Dobrovolsky and the

engineer Georgy Fux. Moscow
Bridge, 816 metres long, is a part of
the North Bridge, six kilometres
long, connecting the right bank
with the new housing district of
the Levoberezhye. Expressive and
original, this suspension bridge
with a 115-metre concrete pylon
is the main high point which is
dominating the low left bank of the
Dnieper.

141. Moscow Bridge

Krasnoarmeiskaya Street. Goloseyevo. Pirogov

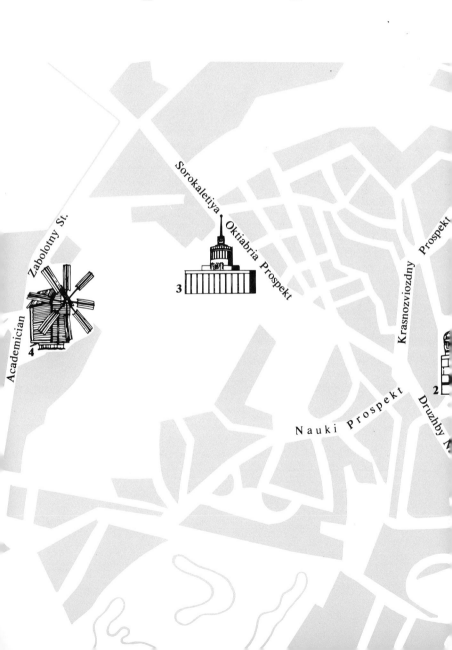

1 The Ukraine Palace of Culture
2 Monument to Cheka soldiers
3 Exhibition of Economic Achievements of the Ukrainian SSR
4 Museum of Folk Architecture and Domestic Life of the Ukrainian SSR

In the first half of the nineteenth century, only the city's outpost was located near Bessarabian Square. The district was beginning to be built up in the 1880s and '90s, when along present-day Krasnoarmeiskaya Street, a natural continuation of Kreshchatik, stone apartment houses began to appear. Traits of eclecticism and the use of Neo-Baroque and Art Nouveau decorative elements were typical of the architectural aspect of these constructions. Contempory buildings, more severe in form, blend in well with the ensemble of the turn of the century.

The spires of two towers of the former **Roman Catholic Church of St. Nicholas** rise over Krasnoarmeiskaya Street. This church of brick and concrete was built in the manner of German Gothic Cathedrals in 1899—1909, by Vladislav Gorodetsky. After restoration in 1978—80, **the House of Organ and Chamber Music** was opened here. Architecturally, *The Ukraine*, **a palace of culture**, is perhaps the central structure of Krasnoarmeiskaya Street. It was built in 1965—70 by Yevgenia Marinchenko, Piotr Zhilitsky, and others. The Palace has a concert hall seating

3,780; its broad stage can hold 1,500 performers. Built of glass and aluminium, it stands on a high foundation. The concave line of the façade and two broad stairways lend it a dynamic quality. The delicate colour-scheme of marble of various sorts on the walls and piers of the main foyer contributes to the elegance of the interior. One of its walls is given over to a large-scale decorative panel, *Birch Grove*, executed in the technique of Florentine mosaic.

142. Palace of Sports, stadium and the hotel Rus

143. The Ukraine Palace of Culture

A monument to Cheka soldiers by Vasily Borodai, sculptor, and Anatoly Ignashchenko, architect, was put up in Dzerzhinsky Square in 1967. The sculpture rises over the modest base, symbolizing the successive generations of the security soldiers.

The continuation of Krasnoarmeiskaya Street is Sorokoletiya Oktiabria (Fortieth-year Anniversary of the October Revolution) Prospekt, which connects the region of Goloseyevsky Park named after Maxim Rylsky with the Exhibition of Economic Achievements of the Ukrainian SSR.

Further south Kitayevo, the site of the country residence of Prince Andrei Bogoliubsky nicknamed Kitai (China), was located. In Kitayevo the remains of the ninth- or tenth-century town have survived, with fortifications and a cave monastery from the time of Kievan Rus. In the seventeenth century, the Kitayev Monastery belonged to the Kievo-Pecherskaya Lavra, and in 1763—67, the Lavra building master Stephen Kovnir erected here the three-aisled five-domed Trinity Church in the Ukrainian Baroque style. It has survived to our day.

144. Roman Catholic
Church of St. Nicholas
(now the House of Organ
and Chamber Music)

143

New buildings for Kiev University are now in course of erection on the other side of Sorokoletiya Oktiabria Prospekt. The project envisages the introduction of the newest construction techniques and materials, with decorative elements — reliefs, mosaic panels and paintings, organically bound to the surrounding landscape.

An autoroute connecting the Exhibition of Economic Achievements with the **Museum of Folk Architecture and Domestic Life of the Ukrainian SSR** runs from Odessa

---

145. Institute of Technical Information

146. Monument to Cheka soldiers

147. One of Kiev University new buildings

148. Exhibition of Economic Achievements of the Ukrainian SSR

Goloseyevo is situated to the west of Kitayevo. A monastery was founded there in the first half of the seventeenth century.

In 1927, the Ukrainian Academy of Agriculture was erected in Goloseyevo by Dmitry Dyachenko, who with great tact and sense of proportion used motifs typical of Ukrainian Baroque.

In the south-west section of Goloseyevo there are pavilions of the **Exhibition of Economic Achievements of the Ukrainian SSR** built by Vladimir Orekhov and a group of architects in 1952—58. These pavilions vividly demonstrate the stylistic tendencies characteristic of the 1950s — the use of purely classical elements blended with decorative motifs of Ukrainian folk art.

Goloseyevsky Park is famous for its thousand-year-old oaks.

Square along Academician Zabolotny Street. The museum is located near the settlement of Pirogov in a region rich in archaeological monuments. Not far from Pirogov, near the village of Khotor, are remains of a fourth-century B.C. Scythian settlement and in the village of Feofania, ramparts of the second to seventh centuries A.D. In Pirogov itself, there are Bronze Age burial sites dating back to 2000 B.C., Slavic settlements from the beginning of our era and of the times of Kievan Rus, and an eleventh- or twelfth-century cave monastery. The green hills and woods, streams and small lakes create ideal surroundings for the display of folk architectural monuments in natural conditions. The opening of the museum took place in 1976.

The nine large sections of the museum give us an ample idea of all the basic ethnographical regions of the Ukraine from the eighteenth to the early twentieth century. The last section, which completes the display, is devoted to the architecture and everyday life of the Soviet socialist village. Each section presents a small settlement with dwelling houses and outbuildings, wells, windmills and wooden churches. Whitewashed huts with tall thatched roofs are surrounded by flower-beds. Within we see a

149—151. Museum of Folk Architecture and Domestic Life of the Ukrainian SSR

furnished room with a rich variety of household objects.

The wooden church of the early seventeenth century transferred to the museum from the village of Doroginka, Kiev District, is distinguished by its laconic form. The well-proportioned silhouette of

another wooden church from the village of Zarubintsy, Cherkassy District, gives a singular note to the rural estate's ensemble. It was built by an unknown building master in 1742. The simple and effective construction consists of three tower-like eight-faceted log structures which are placed on one axis, with three-tiered roof and three cupolas.

In each section the relief of a given locality was taken into account as well as traditional features of the village plan. The museum occupies more than 120 hectares, on which are installed more than 200 constructions, and contains about 40,000 exhibits.

Levoberezhye

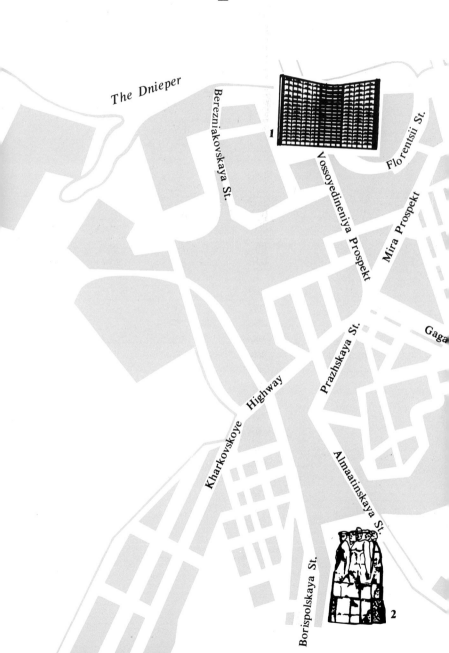

The Dnieper

Berezniakovskaya St.

Vossoyedineniya Prospekt

Florentsii St.

Mira Prospekt

1

Gaga

Prazhskaya St.

Kharkovskoye Highway

Almaatinskaya St.

Borispolskaya St.

2

1   Hotel Slavutich
2   Memorial to Soviet citizens and soldiers killed in the Darnitsa concentration camp in 1941—43

Shestidesiatiletiya Oktiabria Prospekt

ospekt

The historical part of present-day Kiev is the Pravoberezhye. Architectural monuments of the eleventh and twelfth centuries and the art museums are all concentrated there. Even in the early twentieth century, the line dividing Chernigov Province from Kiev Province ran through Trukhanov Island on the Dnieper. The pine woods of the Levoberezhye served as a backdrop for the picturesque face of the city on the Dnieper hills, which rapturous Honoré de Balzac called "Northern Rome". In Soviet times the city has crossed over to the left bank of the Dnieper. In 1923, the city line included the small settlements of the Levoberezhye and the old village of Darnitsa mentioned in the chronicles of the twelfth century. During the Nazi occupation Darnitsa was wiped off the face of the earth. A concentration camp was built in the Darnitsa forest for prisoners of war.

In 1968, on the site of the camp in the heart of the forest, **a memorial to the Soviet citizens and soldiers murdered there in 1941—43** was put up. The entrance is symbolically marked by fragments of barbed wire and chains. In the centre of the meadow on a low hill a sculptural group stands carved out of

150

granite, the work of Valentin Znoba, sculptor, and Alexei Malinovsky and Yury Moskaltsov, architects. A second monument — two
figures of Soviet Army soldiers
cast in bronze, not broken in the
face of death — was placed in the
square in front of the Darnitsa
Railway Station in 1970. This
monument was designed by Vasily
Vinaikin and Victor Grechanik,
sculptors, and Konstantin Sidorov,
architect.

152, 153. Kiev bridges

154, 155. Memorial to Soviet citizens and soldiers murdered by the Nazis in the Darnitsa concentration camp in 1941—43

In the 1960s, construction was begun in the Levoberezhye of new housing estates — Rusanovsky, Berezniaki, Levoberezhny and Voskresensky. The buildings are stretched along the Dnieper for more than eleven kilometres. Among them, rhythmically positioned, are tower-blocks. On the canal between Rusanovsky and Berezniaki 24 powerful fountains create a joyous sight.

Seven bridges unite the Pravoberezhye of the Dnieper with the parks on the islands, the beaches and new living quarters of the Levoberezhye. The lines of Kiev's underground transportation connect the far-flung regions of the left and right banks of the Dnieper. Since 1976 a line of the underground has led from the centre toward Obolon.

Kiev, like a live organism, constantly grows, but the link with the past is never broken. Adherence to tradition makes this link supple and fruitful. Perhaps in urban development more than in any other area of artistic endeavour, moderation in combining the old and the new makes it possible to retain the traditional aspect of a city and at the same time provides it with fresh features. To find this "golden mean" is not easy. This is

156. Hotel Slavutich

especially difficult for those cities
which, like Kiev, are famous for
their unique architectural monuments. The general plan for
Kiev's development takes these
difficulties into consideration. The
face of the city changes every day.
In its new districts, the noise of
construction never ceases: here
foundations are being laid and
roads are being built, there walls
are going up. The city is enlarging
its boundaries. It is not only ex-
panding, it is becoming richer,
more impressive and more beautiful. The buildings of new Kiev by
right stand shoulder to shoulder
with the monuments of the past.

Index

of Streets, Squares and Art Museums
and Monuments Mentioned in the Text

Figures refer to text pages, those in italic
indicate illustrations

КИЕВ

**Архитектурные памятники
и художественные музеи**

Альбом-путеводитель
(на английском языке)

Авторы-составители
Селина Семеновна Гурок,
Борис Борисович Лобановский

Фотографы Р. Б. Бениаминсон,
Ю. М. Бусленко, И. А. Кропивницкий,
Б. А. Миндель, В. А. Моруженко,
Н. Н. Рахманов, В. Б. Соловский,
Т. М. Шабловский, В. И. Шербаков
Перевод с русского А. П. Старос
Оформление Е. А. Лужина
Макет Н. А. Кутового
Редактор Р. П. Клишарова
Редактор английского текста
Э. Г. Андреева
Художественный редактор И. А. Лужина
Технический редактор Н. К. Соколова
Корректор И. Н. Стукалина

ИБ № 1517. Сдано в набор 06.03.86.
Подписано в печать 09.09.86. Формат
60×84 1/16. Бумага мелованная.
Гарнитура таймс. Офсетная печать.
Усл.-печ. л. 9,53. Усл. кр.-отт. 54,17.
Уч.-изд. л. 10,03. Тираж 62 000.
Заказ № 185. Изд. № 3319. Цена 2 р. 80 к.
Издательство «Аврора». 191065, Ленинград,
Невский пр., 7/9
Типография В/О «Внешторгиздат»
при Государственном комитете СССР
по делам издательств, полиграфии и книжной
торговли. 127576, Москва, Илимская ул., 7

Printed and bound in the USSR